What others have said about Bob's Message

Bob Anderson carries a message that is vitally important to successful recovery from alcoholism. He is a gifted teacher who has had a major impact on my life. He teaches from a deep spiritual understanding and has provided a path for recovery for countless suffering alcoholics. I can recommend Bob Anderson to everyone whose life has been affected by alcoholism.

- ***Lloyd Hyndman M.D.*** **Medical Director & Staff Psychiatrist, Drug & Alcohol Services & Department of Mental Health Services**

I was introduced to Bob Anderson through cassettes given to me by a friend. When I listened to his presentation I found it incredible that Bob Anderson, a layman, comprehended and was able to apply the most modern and fundamental principles of psychological thinking to such an extent that his communication could be curative. His genius is that it reaches and can reach all people at the deep level of their defense mechanisms. Exposure of the fundamental nature of these defenses produces acceptance so that the individual's thinking, character and behavior are transformed. The results of his message are dramatic and in reality is the basis of all therapies. These ideas are of value to all that are in the field of mental health and especially alcoholism and addiction. My 45 years of psychoanalytic practice enables me to appreciate and embrace the wonderful gift Bob Anderson brings to us by sharing his thoughts.

- ***Carolyn A. Hays M.D.*** **Psychoanalyst, Beverly Hills, California**

In my late 30's I became a homeless alcoholic and eventually a severe crack addict. After 7 years of homelessness, several trips to mental hospitals and countless visits with psychiatrists and therapists, I surrendered to the help of a treatment center, sobered up and was put on several medications. However, I still had paralyzing bouts of depression. I wondered if I would have to settle for a life of depression, medications and 12 Step meetings. At 18 months sober, I heard Bob Anderson's message in a Twelve Step meeting. My first reaction was "Wow, the last thing that I am learning is the first thing that I needed to know". From application of the program as taught by Bob Anderson, my life improved and has improved ever since. I was able to go off medications and start working. I have my own apartment. I have a sense of calmness and peace of mind that I have never known was possible.

- ***Sherry Smith,* Upland, California**

In 1977, I got sober through a recovery home and 12 Step meetings. I was told to get a sponsor, work the steps, don't drink no matter what, go to meetings and eventually I would be a winner. I desperately wanted to stay sober so I followed direction. After hearing problems after problems in meetings, I believed the way I thought and acted was normal. I switched from obsession to obsession. At five years sober, I married my night in shining armor and started a family. At 16 years sober, I was heading for a divorce. I was very confused and depressed. I heard something from Bob Anderson that I desperately needed. He described alcoholism as a mind-powered disease. I did not even know that my years of sobriety were characterized by untreated alcoholism. I finally comprehended what was wrong and found a way of life that has enabled me to become happily and usefully whole as a way of life.

- ***Jenny Adamo,* Manhattan Beach, California**

In July 1976, I was introduced to Bob. He led me, guided me and educated me in the process of getting sober. Bob's message about his life, alcoholism and the recovery process can be understood by anyone and encompasses a design for living in which substance abuse is not necessary to enjoy life. My life has never been fuller or broader in nature.

- ***Melvin Wellstead,* Denver, Colorado**

I am an alcoholic and drug addict. I came from a very fast, hard and dangerous life. People who know me are amazed that I am still alive. By the grace of God, I got sober in a rehabilitation hospital and have remained sober ever since. Although sober, active and attending many different 12 Step meetings for the first 2 ½ years of recovery, I still did not understand what was wrong with me. I was very unhappy and even became suicidal. Fortunately, I met Bob Anderson. Even though English is not my native language, Bob spoke in such a way that I could understand what was wrong and what to do about it. My life has completely changed ever since. I am so very grateful to Bob for making this message available to me.

- ***Ali Mosavi,* Hollywood, California**

A Mind-Powered Disease

Recognizing and Treating Alcoholism
to Find Success in Life
Through the 12 Step Program

By Bob Anderson
with Sylvie Gabriele

a PRIMETIME RECOVERY book
published by Intellective Media

Other products by Primetime Recovery include audiocassettes and videocassettes of Bob Anderson.

For a free catalog or ordering information:

Visit our website: www.primetimerecovery.com

Call: Within the USA (866) 4-Recovery; outside the USA (310) 802-0215

Write: Primetime Recovery, P.O. Box 2035, Manhattan Beach, CA 90266-2035

The Twelve Steps, Twelve Steps and Twelve Traditions, Alcoholics Anonymous, The Language of the Heart and Alcoholics Anonymous Comes of Age have been reprinted and adapted with permission of Alcoholics Anonymous World Services, Inc. The opinions expressed are not to be attributed to Alcoholics Anonymous, nor does *A Mind-Powered Disease: Recognizing and Treating Alcoholism to Find Success in Life through the Twelve Step Program* imply any endorsement of Alcoholics Anonymous. No copyright is claimed to *The Twelve Steps, Twelve Steps and Twelve Traditions, Alcoholics Anonymous, The Language of the Heart and Alcoholics Anonymous Comes of Age*. However, copyright is claimed in the compilation, selection, coordination and/or arrangement of such material herein.

Published by Intellective Media Incorporated, P.O. Box 2035, Manhattan Beach, CA 90266-2035.

Printed in the United States of America.
Production by Resource Graphics, San Jose California.

Library of Congress Card Catalog Number:
Gabriele, Sylvie. A Mind-Powered Disease.
ISBN 0-9704826-0-4

To Bob, who unconditionally dedicated his life to helping others recover. He never gave up on his purpose and he never gave up on those he helped. This book is a tribute to Bob. May he always be proud of us and may he always know how much we love him.

To Nicolaus, for his unconditional encouragement and support.

To Ali, for his deep commitment and support of Bob and me.

To my family, who makes my life richer every day with their support and love.

To all our friends, who believe in Bob and keep this message alive.

Please be aware

This book is designed to provide information on alcoholism and the Twelve Step Program of Recovery and contains strictly the opinion of the authors based on their personal experience. It is sold with the understanding that the publisher and author are not 1) engaged in rendering professional medical, behavioral or psychological advice, 2) to be the sole source of assistance on the subject of alcoholism, addiction, other obsessive-compulsive behaviors and recovery from these afflictions and 3) to be a substitute for hospitalization, detoxification and rehabilitation. If professional assistance is required, the services of a competent professional should be sought.

Contents

Letter to the Reader

Thank you for your interest in this book. My hope is that you will find the happiness and peace of mind that I found through hearing and applying the message carried by Bob Anderson. As I will share in my story, the moment I heard Bob's message my whole life turned around. Bob was my sponsor and best friend. He gave me everything he had so I could find a good life. Through a willing and persistent effort, I found a beautiful new life, one day at a time. The inspiration I have to cowrite *A Mind-Powered Disease* with Bob is to make available the message that God and Bob graciously made available to me. I encourage you to read and keep reading this message. I assure you, you have struck gold. Do not throw it away. If I can impart a few words of wisdom, please consider my suggestions as you read this book.

Be sure to keep an open mind. I delayed my own progress by having a closed mind. For instance, don't let yourself be critical of the way Bob carries this message. He is intentionally repetitive because the disease is repetitive. Your mind can and will leave the page and miss what has been written. So Bob repeats himself to ensure that the message is delivered. Bob also uses the English language in a variety of ways. He may speak with foreign idioms and slang or he may switch between grammatical casualty and proper English. Bob is deliberately repetitive and variable as he reaches a diverse audience. Therefore, keep an open mind. Bob's method of delivery should not interfere with your receptiveness to the message.

Furthermore, because the mind has the power to leave the page and miss the message, keep reading this book over and over again. As you change, the message in this book will deepen. Each day these words will take on new meaning. What you read today may and will be different from what you read yesterday. Therefore, keep this message alive by reading it over and over again.

Lastly, in the beginning I was able to listen to Bob, hear and learn his words and agree with what he said, and still have untreated alcoholism. But I missed the whole program because the way of life in the program of recovery depends on *the application* of the words as a way of life, not on intelligence. I cannot learn this way of life and graduate because that is not how the disease works. Therefore, I urge you never to get too "smart." Make a willing and persistent effort to see how the Twelve Steps apply to your life daily.

May God bless you and keep you until then,

Sylvie

Preface

Bob's Story

A *Mind-Powered Disease* brings together a series of audiocassette recordings from a retreat conducted by Bob Anderson. The following is a brief introduction to Bob. More about Bob will be found throughout this book.

On December 11, 1952, Bob entered an alcoholic hospital in Cleveland, Ohio. On December 13, 1952, he was released from the hospital. This date marks his sobriety anniversary.

At two-and-a-half-years sober, Bob realized that he was in a serious dilemma—that is, he was the same man sober as he was drunk. Although sober he thought and acted the same way. He was still mean and mad. He also realized that no matter how hard he tried or how much he vowed to change, he repeated the same performance. He was still irritable, restless, and discontented. He was not happy, joyous, and free in the day he was in. Nobody ever explained to him the disease of alcoholism and that lack of power is his dilemma. They would say, "Keep coming back; eventually you'll become a winner." They would talk about how they lost their houses, their jobs, or whatever they lost and how they got new houses, their jobs back, or whatever else, but nobody would talk about the in-between. Nobody would describe how the alcoholic mind functioned and how untreated alcoholism manifested into an unmanageable life. On his own, Bob began a search for an answer to this dilemma. Through trial and error, he found the answer. He became aware of how alcoholism, ego, and self functioned in the day he was in. He found that the alcoholic lacks the power to live to good purpose because he lost the power of choice in thinking, not just in drinking. He also found a way of life in which he could treat this disease and change, daily, through the application of the Twelve Step Recovery Program.

Once Bob found this way of life, he devoted himself to teaching the Twelve Step Program of Recovery by creating awareness about the nature of alcoholism as a mind-powered disease and by teaching about the Twelve Steps as a way of life. During his forty-four years of sobriety, Bob helped countless sufferers, families, friends, and others all over the world by conducting numerous meetings, workshops, and three-day retreats. These meetings, workshops, and retreats were recorded. Although these works were recorded, Bob has never published them in print until this present volume.

In 1994, Bob and Sylvie established PRIMETIME RECOVERY, an organization dedicated to creating awareness about the true nature of the disease of alcoholism as a mind-powered disease and to educate sufferers, families, friends, and others on the Twelve Step method for recovery through books and audio and video media. Bob remained sober and active until the day he passed away — April 16, 1997. PRIMETIME RECOVERY continues to help others through Bob's message by reproducing and distributing his works worldwide.

To contact PRIMETIME RECOVERY, visit our website, www.primetimerecovery.com; call (866) 4-RECOVERY, (866) 473-2683, (310) 802-0215; or write PRIMETIME RECOVERY, P.O. Box 2035, Manhattan Beach, CA 90266-2035.

Preface

Sylvie's Story

As I mentioned, I was inspired to do this book with Bob because his message turned my life around. Even though my story is not much different from so many others', for the sake of those who are interested, I will share what it was like, what happened, and what it is like for me now. However, because Bob so eloquently explains the nature of alcoholism and the method of recovery, I will leave that discussion to him in the chapters of this book.

In 1992, I identified as an alcoholic and became a member of the Twelve Step Recovery Program. I was a periodic alcoholic before I got into recovery, which means that I would go on drinking binges at different periods of my life.

At thirteen years old I began to drink with my friends from middle school. I enjoyed the effect produced by alcohol the first time I got drunk. I found that alcohol gave me a sense of ease that I was not able to achieve sober. It made me feel smarter and prettier than everyone else. I felt capable of doing things that I could never do before. For the first time I felt a part of the world. I found that I could use alcohol to help me fit in. The way of life produced by alcohol made everything exciting and fun, except that I had to hide and lie to live it.

I would lie to my parents. I would stay out all night drinking and partying. I drank at school, at home, and with my friends. Also, I found I could steal what I wanted. I stole money from my parents. I stole alcohol from grocery stores. I stole clothes and jewelry from clothing stores. I also found boys. I did not know that the disease of alcoholism was beginning to set in. I thought the way I was living was all in "good fun."

At seventeen years old, I realized my friends were going to college and I couldn't because my grades were not good enough. I was crushed. I was also very jealous and did not like others being ahead of me, so I got serious about school. I still drank on the weekends and had obsessive relationships with guys. As I tried to do better in school, I competed with everyone. I made my friends feel like dirt when they got better grades than I did. I would always play favorites and then turn. At one point, my friends all warned me that if I didn't change, they would no longer be my friends. I stopped being openly mean, but I couldn't stop being mean and mad inside.

At eighteen years old I started junior college and found a new boyfriend. With all the determination I could muster, I locked myself into my bedroom and studied all the time. I isolated from my friends, I fought with my boyfriend all the time, and I continued to drink on the weekends. Finally, my mother pushed me into psychotherapy, in which I willingly stayed for five years. I would go every week for five years. Most of the time I would be depressed. I was always unsatisfied. I never thought I was going anywhere. But at the same time, I thought I was making progress. I identified my feelings and learned to communicate them in hopes they would diffuse. I also became assertive and broke up with my boyfriend.

At twenty years old, after spending two years at a junior college and making a 3.7 grade point average, I got accepted to UCLA. In the meantime, I continued to drink. At twenty-three years old, I graduated with a bachelor's degree in psychology. I continued contentious, but close, friendships with my high school girlfriends. My relationships were still obsessive. Inside I was still the same. People irritated me. They made me mad, but the difference was that I could communicate with them. I was getting worse. I did not know that my friendships with others were always conditional. As long as they did what I wanted, I would accept them. If not, I would blow and then tell them why I was angry. I could not accept people for the way they were. I always wanted to change them. I did not know my alcoholism had progressed. Deep inside, I am sure people could not understand how moody I was. I assume they were relieved that I was in therapy.

When I graduated from UCLA, I decided that my life was on track and no longer needed therapy, so my therapist and I decided we would discontinue our relationship. For graduation, my parents gave me a trip to Europe, so three girlfriends and I went. Before the trip, my mother and her fiance asked me to attend Twelve Step meetings with them. I decided to go because I was in therapy and thought I could benefit.

On the trip, we drank every day. We shopped every day. We ate McDonalds every day. I searched for Romeo every day. We drank non stop cappuccinos (caffeine rush) every day. But somehow I was getting more and more restless, irritable, and discontented. On the outside I had everything going for me, but on the inside I was miserable. Everything irritated me. My friends irritated me more and more. In my mind I was stuck with them for ten weeks and the trip was supposed to be fun. This scenario was typical for me. I could never think, feel, and be like I was supposed to be. I always looked at the downside of things. I tried to talk with my friends but they looked at me as though something was really wrong. I could not find an excuse for myself. Not only was I miserable on the inside, but I also could not drink another cappuccino, I could not purchase another thing, I could not find my Romeo, and I gained weight from McDonalds. By the end of the trip, something very strange happened. I would drink and drink and I could no longer get drunk anymore. No matter how much I drank, I was conscious the whole time. Everyone else was having fun and I wasn't. Somehow I lost something inside me and I could not get drunk. I felt doomed. I had no where to go. I could not escape myself. I became desperate. I did not know that my alcoholism had progressed. At twenty-three years old, I hit bottom. I did not hit bottom by losing homes, cars, family, or friends or by getting DUIs or the like. I hit bottom in my mind. I lost confidence in my own judgment, I could not think clearly, and I could not run to the bottle. I lost my friends' confidence in me, and I was desperate inside. I did not know where to turn. So I returned to my therapist, who was a sober member of a Twelve Step Program. I asked her what happened. I desperately needed her to tell me what was wrong with me. She didn't. So I gave up on therapy. By the grace of God, I had begun to attend these Twelve Step meetings and felt comfortable there. I actually felt like I belonged.

So I stayed. While attending meetings, people would talk about being alcoholic. They said to "never pick up the first drink." They told me to "keep coming back, turn it over, and eventually I would be a winner." I did not know what "turn it over" meant or how to do it. I moaned and groaned and they said, "That's the committee" or "That's stinking thinking." I asked what that meant. I could not get a straight answer. I could not see that I had a problem. I could not see that my track record was characteristic of alcoholism. I did not know what was wrong with me until the day I met Bob. I was one year sober. The first time I heard him speak, I knew he had the answer. I finally found out what was wrong with me and what to do about it. By the grace of God and Bob and through a willing and persistent effort, I have changed and I continue to change, daily. My life gets fuller and brighter each day. I went back to school to achieve a Masters in Business Administration from Loyola Marymount University in Los

Angeles. I am happily married with a man who shares this way of life with me, and I have a prosperous career. Most importantly, I finally feel happily and usefully whole. Since I found this message, I have devoted my life to helping others to find this way of life, which is outlined in this book.

Part 1

Relapse Prevention

Introduction

The ABCs of Alcoholism

I'm Bob, an alcoholic.

To get this retreat started, I'd like to tell you a little about how I found the Twelve Steps. I met the man who became my sponsor in a beer joint. He was an ice man, delivering ice to this joint. In those days, they used to bring in the ice and put it in the cooler. When he finished, he'd come around and sit alongside of me. He never once talked to me about my life, how bad off I was, or what I was doing wrong. But I heard through the bartenders and the owners of this joint that he used to be like I was, but he had changed. And, then, there came a time when my life crashed. Even though I had only known him in the bar, I yelled for help. He put me in the hospital where they strapped me to a bed and filled me with paraldehyde.

And that's when my life started.

The only reason I'm telling you what happened is so you'll know that I belong in this Twelve Step Program of Recovery. I didn't know that right away, of course. I thought my life had ended instead of just begun.

I spent three-and-a-half months in Cleveland, Ohio, working with my sponsor. Every day, when he got through with his work, he would bang on my door and away we'd go. He didn't call me, he didn't ask me if I wanted to go, he'd just say "Let's go" and away we'd go. I'd go with him to drying-out places, to meetings, to Twelve Step calls, and everything. I was along for the ride. I had no idea what I was doing, other than not drinking.

After three-and-a-half months, I had to leave Ohio and come out to California because my wife was sick. For the next two-and-a-half years, I remained the same sober as I was drunk. I thought the name of the game was going to meetings, staying sober, and doing the best you can with what you have.

But I didn't know what was wrong with me.

I didn't know the disease of alcoholism. They never talked about the disease of alcoholism in meetings. For a long time, I couldn't identify anything in my life or in my behavior with what they were saying in these meetings. I didn't know what was going on. I just didn't know. But I kept going to meetings and I kept hearing about things that didn't relate to my life. People would give their drunkalogues, or talk about how everything was cool since they joined the Twelve Step Program of Recovery, or talk about how they had the good life or whatever. I struggled with finding the good life. I was really fighting the world. All I had was me because I never gave no prayer to no God at no time. See, I wasn't hooked up at all. I was fighting, denying, and doing things I shouldn't have been doing. I couldn't couple up the way I lived with why I was in a Twelve Step program. I just couldn't do it. But I kept going to meetings. And I would hear them say, "Go to more meetings," "Stay sober," "Read the Big Book," "Put the Steps in your life," and so on.

I had a sponsor. At the time, I thought I could listen and do what he was telling me to do. We would sit for hours after hours after hours talking about the Steps. All of that time, one thing was missing out of my mind. A sense of a power greater than myself. At the time, I hadn't even begun to realize that I was a power. That came later. In the meantime, the disease of alcoholism was being displayed in my life, at my work, in the way I drove my car, in the way I talked to my wife. I would get mean, mad, and hostile. I figured I had the right to do what I was doing because I was sober. I figured being sober was what it was all about.

Now I know that I was the same sober as I was drunk. In fact, I was worse. Every day, sober, I would get stronger and do more damage. I didn't know that this was the disease of alcoholism. That's what was happening to my mind a long time ago, and it's still there. My mind controls me. It talks to me. It tells me things. I listen to it. When I'm sober, I think I have the ability to not get mad, to not look at you cock-eyed, to not hate your guts. And it isn't so.

That's the way it is with the disease of alcoholism. It's a mind-controlling disease. Back then, because I was sober, I was able to work steady. I started acquiring things. Trouble was, the more I got the meaner I got. The disease was progressing. My mind had greater strength and I thought I had greater control, so I never gave a desperation prayer to no God at no time. I didn't have one. I didn't even know what it was like to pray.

All I had was a sponsor who was a Step man and a God man. He was always talking about the grace of God. That was his life, though. That's what he used. That's what he did. I thought I could do what he said because I listened to him. I thought, "This is good stuff." But there was no way I could do what he said or did. The disease wouldn't let me. I was still angry inside. I was still carrying that chip on my shoulder. I was still fighting the world. I was looking at a world that was just as ratty as it was when I was drunk.

I would go to a meeting and hear somebody talk about what they had lost. Now they're sober, now they've put the Steps into their life, and they've got a good life. And I'm thinking, "This is wonderful stuff." And I leave the meeting. But I don't leave the meeting with that guy. I leave the meeting with me, and I'm still the same. So here I am, back in the same world. I know this world sober and I know it drunk. It's the same world. It hasn't changed. Not a bit.

Now when I came into the Twelve Step Program of Recovery, I heard about the Steps right away. I had a sponsor who pounced on me. But the disease of alcoholism kept telling me I was going to be all right. But I wasn't all right. I thought that if I kept going to Twelve Step meetings, I would eventually become a winner. Well, it never happened because I wasn't a winner. I was the same sober as I was drunk.

Right from the word "go," as soon as I got to California, I was picking up babies, making Twelve Step calls. Someone would call me up because I was going to meetings and was sober. "Would you make a Twelve Step call on somebody?" Now what kind of Twelve Step call could I make on somebody? The best I could do was take them to meetings with me, which I did. But I'm still doing everything the same way I did before. I think staying sober is the best I can do and staying sober is what this program is all about.

That's not what it's all about. My head is wrong. My mind is wrong. I mean well and I'm sober, but I can't do well. I don't know why I can't do well. I try to figure out how to say things. I try to look at things and people to figure out what's best. How do I respond when somebody attacks me? How do I respond when I'm on the freeway and somebody tries to run me off the road? What do I do? What do I do? I don't know what to do. So I do what I think is best and that behavior is the same thing that brought me here. I don't know how to do anything else. I don't know how to not get mad. I don't know how to not do the things that make me sick inside. I look at my wife like everything she does is wrong. She says something and it makes me mad. I want to show her she's wrong, and I don't know why. This is the disease of alcoholism.

I don't care who you are. I think you're at fault. You drive your car wrong and that entitles me to think that you're all wet. I can watch a guy park a car, and I'll think, "Isn't that terrible? He doesn't even know how to park that car." How he parks his car hasn't got a thing to do with my life, but what he's doing upsets me. I think it's okay to get upset, it's okay to burn and boil because of other people's behavior. When I'm like that, everything I look at is wrong. I've got something happening to me, and I don't know what it is. It's the same thing that would happen to me when I was drinking and getting drunk. Here I am sober and now it's the same thing again. I can't stand people. I've got a dissatisfied mind.

Nothing pleases me. Nothing. In 1954, I bought a brand-new Mercury, right off the showroom. First I think, this life is wonderful. Here I got a brand-new car. I'm really doing well. And then I can't even drive the thing. I try to drive and I get mad. I get mean. People blow their horns at me and I think, "Don't they know who I am?" Of course, they don't know who I am. And I get mad about it. And it bothers me, but I don't know why.

We have to talk about the disease of alcoholism. If my disease isn't treated by the program of recovery, I'll do the same thing today as I did yesterday. My disease will make me restless, irritable, discontented. I'll find fault.

My mind is hurt. My mind is injured. And this mind is in me. How can I think that the name of the game is staying sober when I've got a mind that can't be satisfied? The disease of alcoholism centers in the mind, not the body. On page 23 of the Big Book it says, "it would be pointless and academic to talk about the troubles alcohol produces if we never took the first drink, thereby setting the terrible cycle in motion. Therefore, the main problem of the alcoholic centers in his mind, rather than his body." You see, alcoholism has nothing to do with bottles, bars, or alcohol. I got a mind that tells me you're wrong and I'm right. That's not alcohol, but it is alcoholism.

In the Big Book on page 60, it says, "The first requirement is that we be convinced that any life run on self-will can hardly be a success." I am always in conflict, always arguing, always fighting something or somebody even when my motives are good. But I don't think that's me because I'm sober. I think I'm a good guy. I'm sober. I'm buying a house, a car. I'm helping my wife. I'm helping my neighbor. But in the next minute, I'm ready to kill you. I don't know what that is. I can't put it together. I'm always against you. I'm always against everything. I don't care what it is, I'm going to find fault with it. I'm going to look at you, and I'm going to find fault. I'm going to tell you everything about you that I think is wrong with you.

This is how I think, and it upsets me. That's the disease of alcoholism. I think I can change something and make it right, but I can't. I think I can do it because I think it's you that's not right. I don't know that it's me.

I'm a self-talker. I'm sober, I go to meetings. I've learned about steps. I found a God, and I even pray to God. But I still talk to myself. My mind talks to me and tells me how things should be. When they are not that way, it bothers me. I have a mind that tells me exactly how wrong you are. I listen to this mind. This mind is where the disease is. This mind is what I brought here. This is the mind that I drank with, and now I'm still talking to myself the same way I did when I was drunk. "I don't like this." "I don't like that." "This should be different." "That should be different." This mind is a self-talking mind, but it talks with power. It tells me what to do, how to do it, when to do it, and where to do it.

I want you to behave. I won't accept you for who you are. I just won't do it. I want you to change because I want you to change. It's like this with my wife, the same way. When I look at her, I want her to do different than she does. But she doesn't know this, so she doesn't do different and I get upset. She can't do different. How could she? I'm the one that thinks she should do different, not her. And I can't accept this. I can't even look at it.

This thinking affects every part of my life. When I'm working with a guy, I don't think he's doing a good job. I figure, "He's dumb. He's nuts. He doesn't know what he's doing." And it bothers me. It upsets me. It's the same thing when I drive my car. Why can't I drive my car without driving your car? Everything you're doing in that car is wrong, the way I look at it.

This is the way I live in all of my affairs if my alcoholism is not treated. In the Big Book on page 85 it says, "We are not cured of alcoholism. What we really have is a daily reprieve contingent on the maintenance of our spiritual condition …." Today my spiritual condition is not very good. I still can't drive my car without driving your car.

The Steps are not numbers, they are a way of life. The program of recovery is not about whether you go to a lot of meetings or no meetings, or whether you do a lot of praying or no praying. Even those things don't stop the disease of alcoholism. They do not stop the disease. But I don't know this. I figure if I go to a lot of meetings, I can handle things a little better. I can be more careful. I won't blow my lid so hard. I won't get so mad at somebody. And the next thing, you know what happens? I get madder than I ever got at somebody.

My mind is a power that I use, but it's not a higher power, a power greater than me. It's my power. For my whole life, even after I joined the Twelve Step program, the same power controlled my life. It was me. It's my mind. It's the way I think. I get restless, irritable, and discontented. Dr. William D. Silkworth, in the Big Book, talks about how "men and women drink essentially because they like the effect produced by alcohol. The sensation is so elusive that, while they admit it is injurious, they cannot after time differentiate the true from the false. To them, their alcoholic life seems the only normal one. They are restless, irritable, and discontented, unless they again experience the sense of ease and comfort which comes at once by taking a few drinks—drinks which they see others taking with impunity"(xxvi). What he's telling me is that this alcohol was treating my alcoholism, and I didn't even know it. Alcohol created a world I could live in, a world where I wasn't finding fault, where my mind said everything was cool. There wasn't a fight going on because I was fogged. Alcohol was taking care of my disease.

After I got to the Twelve Step program and I quit drinking booze, how was I going to handle the same mind that brought me here? What am I going to do with this mind? I went for two years in this Twelve Step program fighting everything and everybody, every day. I lived in the same world drunk as I did sober. Nothing really had changed. I'm restless, irritable, and discontented. Not because of alcohol but because of alcoholism.

I didn't know that my yesterdays, whether I was drunk or sober, are my todays and my future, all the time. I'll do again the same things today as I did yesterday. If my alcoholism doesn't get treated, if I'm without a program of recovery and this here power they call God, I'm going to have to do everything again, and again, and again, and again. I kept looking backwards and I kept looking forwards, thinking that I was going to get better if I went to more meetings, if I got a sponsor, and if I did more Steps. I thought, "I have a long way to go but, after so many years, I'm going to be okay." Now that was the disease talking. What my mind is telling me isn't real. It isn't going to happen that way. I don't have a long way to go. I have only the now, only the moment I'm in, right now. I'm an alcoholic with alcoholism. There's no such thing as tomorrows because I am sick today. I do damage today. It don't kill me tomorrow. It don't kill me yesterday. It's killing me now. The disease of alcoholism has to be looked at. It has to be considered.

What is the disease of alcoholism? It's an alive thing. It's an "ism," not a "wasm." You can't treat it until it's gone. You can't say, "I've gone to ten meetings this week. I'm okay now. Now I can do anything I want." You can't do that. Why? Because the moment you do the same thing you used to do, you'll get the same result. Now that's a hard nut to swallow, but it's in the Steps and it's the truth. If you don't think so, look at your track record. Look at today, this day, today. Is there anything that went on today that upset you, that you didn't like, that you wanted different? Is there anything that you thought of today that makes you feel guilty or uncomfortable? Did you answer somebody the wrong way and then later on wish to heck you never answered them that way? You must ask yourself these questions.

These are questions I never wanted to consider. I always put the blame elsewhere, thinking I was entitled to behave the way I did because I was sober, I was a member of a Twelve Step program, and I had a lot of years in the program. My mind was always saying, "They're wrong. I'm special, and they didn't treat me the way they should." This behavior could have occurred at the airport, a restaurant, anywhere, maybe with someone I loved. This is the disease of alcoholism. It's still in me. It's never cured. As I read before on page 85 of the Big Book, it says, "We are not cured of alcoholism. What we really have is a daily reprieve contingent on the maintenance of our spiritual condition. Every day is a day when we must carry the vision of God's will into all of our activities."

I've been sober for forty-four years. But today, this day, now, I must have the same thing that any alcoholic coming through the door must have. I must have my alcoholism treated right now. Now. Now. Now. Not tonight. Not after the retreat. Not after I learn more. The disease will tell me that I can get away with anything because I have a long way to go, because I'm new, because I don't have the Twelve Steps in my life. But alcoholism isn't treated that way. Alcoholism must be treated in the moment you're in.

I don't know if you buy what I'm saying. I didn't buy it when I was first sober. I thought if I did this or got more of that, my program of recovery would come along sometime in the future. I don't know how you think about it, but that's how I thought about it.

My sponsor had nine years. His birthday was in December 1943. He had nine years when I yelled for help. He put me in a hospital. When I got out, I thought that I'd be like him when I got nine years. That's what I used to tell him. When he talked about the Steps, I'd say, "Steve, when I get nine years, I'll know what you know and I'll be doing exactly what you're doing now." And he'd say, "No, no, it's not the quantity of years, it's the quality." Now I didn't know what he was talking about. It just didn't make any sense. But today, I know what he meant. He meant that this disease has to be treated now, today, or it was never going to be treated. So I'm telling you the same thing. When you wake up in the morning, as an alcoholic with alcoholism, if you don't start your program of recovery right then, you haven't got one.

Now how'd you like to have somebody tell you that after you got some years? How would you like to hear that? I didn't like it. It didn't make any sense at all. Back in those days, I had been real busy in the program and I thought, "Well, aren't you going to give me some credit? Aren't you going to recognize all the things I've been doing in the program? Doesn't that count? Don't those yesterdays count?" No, they don't count. They don't. They don't really count. The disease has to be treated now. You can't store this stuff up. You can't store up your time, or your prayers, or your meetings, or your Twelve Step work. When you get in trouble, you can't draw from an account, like you do a bank account, as if your yesterdays are going to take care of today's thinking.

What I'm talking about now has to be presented. What I'm talking about is food and you have to eat it. You can look at it all you want and it'll never do you a bit of good. You'll starve to death if you don't eat it. It's the same principle, the same thing. If I don't put it inside of me, if I don't use it, I can't benefit from it. This recovery program is serious. It is prime time. Prime time means the very best. It can be no better. There's no other place to go. The program of recovery hasn't changed since its conception. It's the same. It's the same program of recovery. They are the same Steps that I started with and my sponsor started with.

This is an application of principles. What's an application? It's not a reading thing, it's not a discussing thing. An application is a doing thing. This is in print. It's written in the *Big Book*, the *Twelve by Twelve*, *The Language of The Heart*, *The Sermon on the Mount*, or Dr. Tiebout's papers. I'm not saying this is what I believe because it helped me only. I'm saying these things because they helped me but that's because they were already in print. These principles are already established. What I'm saying is all true. So it's a message. It's a message about recovery through the Twelve Steps.

Why do each and every one of us have to have this message? Because we have the disease of alcoholism. The Big Book was printed for alcoholics with alcoholism to treat their alcoholism. It was not created for mankind, like the Bible was. The Big Book is for alcoholics. Mankind doesn't have the trouble we have. We're bodily and mentally different. In Chapter 3 of the Big Book, its says, "No person likes to think that he is bodily and mentally different from his fellows. Therefore, it is not surprising that our drinking careers have been characterized by countless vain attempts to prove we could drink like other people. The idea that somehow, someday he will control and enjoy his drinking is the great obsession of every abnormal drinker" (30).

This message is saving my life today. It's giving me a world that I never knew existed. I never knew that you could have a day so pleasing, where all good things come to you without having to look for 'em. I didn't know that because I fought everything. I pushed and shoved and fought people. And I mean I fought 'em to prove a point or to get something. And I kept losing all the time. Here I am, sober, and I'm still losing. I'm losing my mind. I'm losing my friends. I'm losing my self-respect. When I was drinking, I lived in the sewer and lost everything. Now I'm in a Twelve Step program and I'm still losing. I think maybe more meetings will treat my disease, but attending meetings will never change my character. Meetings are essential. I'm not putting them down. Meetings are a must for every one of us. For me, too. Reading is essential, too. But these don't change character. You can put this book down and not one word you've read will do you any good. This information won't change your character.

The Twelve Step program has two ingredients. First, there's a power, a power in the Steps. The power is a power greater than me, and this power turns out to be God. That's what this message is all about. It's about a power called God. He's the Lord of my life. But there's another ingredient: there are the Twelve Steps. There's a method of living, with a power behind it that makes it possible to live that method. This method is about building a new character. I cannot be who I am, I cannot stay the way I am and have any success. I have to change. This is the message right now. This message isn't about going to meetings. It is to learn about my character. The character that I brought here, me. This character that I brought here cannot act any differently than it ever did. Therefore, being sober isn't the name of the game. Being sober is a requirement, but it's not the name of the game.

At one time I didn't know that. I still thought I'm eventually going to get it. I just have to go to more meetings. I just have to do certain things. Well, no way. If you're like me, you're going to sink. You're not going to make it. After two-and-a-half years in this program, I was doing things I said I would never do again. When I was drunk, I had a legitimate excuse. When I was drunk, I used to tell my wife, "I'll never do that again. I'm sorry. I was drunk. I didn't know any better." I'd tell my boss the same thing so he wouldn't fire me. But here I am sober. I don't have any excuse. I can't say I hit my wife because I was sober. That doesn't make sense. I didn't understand. My character was doing the same old things because I was the same old character. I haven't changed. I just don't have the drunken behavior, that's all. My mind is just as ratty. My mind still goes in the sewer without a program of recovery because, without it, I can't change. This program is a program of recovery. It is not a program of failure. It is not a program that works just for me and not for you. This program is a program of recovery for every alcoholic. It is a program that will change your character.

I had to hang on to that word for a long time because I didn't like that word. Character. When I was younger, everybody referred to me as a bad character.

"Don't trust that *character*."

"That *character* will turn on you."

"That *character* fights all the time."

"Don't go out with that *character*."

People were always calling me a character. Then when I got here, everybody was talking about my character. The literature talked about character. The steps talked about character. So I think, there's no way I'm going to look at that word. There's no way I wanted to look at my character. But they talk about character in the program of recovery.

In *Twelve Steps and Twelve Traditions*, it says that "we had lacked the perspective to see that character building and spiritual values had to come first, and that material satisfactions were not the purpose of living" (71). Alcoholism must be talked about so there is a purpose to the Steps. The Steps are in a logical order, from one to twelve, for the treatment of alcoholism. Step One starts to build a new character now.

Don't put this information away. Don't say the words, store them away, and think you can do something because you heard a few words. Sometimes I have to hear something a hundred times. I might even hear only half of it after a hundred times. I got a brain that goes anywhere it wants to go. The body stays here but the brain takes off. Think about it. While you've been reading this book, how many times has your brain left the page? I used to go to meetings and, especially when I was running real heavy with the gals, my mind would take off. I'll bet you two-to-one that my mind wasn't at those meetings for more than five minutes.

This message saved my life. Alcoholism was never treated before the Twelve Steps came along. This program was put on this earth to treat alcoholism. Think about what I'm saying. This program was put on this earth to treat alcoholism. Why? Because if you treat my alcoholism the way it should be treated, with God and the Steps, then my whole life changes. My whole being is different. I'm a new character. I can contribute something to the world today. Before I found the Twelve Steps, I used to take all the time. I was always looking after me, hurting you. Whoever you were, it didn't make any difference. Today the picture is turning around.

This life that I'm in today is a different world entirely. There is only one world, but there are two concepts. I lived in one concept, which was me. The other concept is God's world. This is a world that I want to live in today. For a long time, even sober, I couldn't live in it. I couldn't even live in God's world for a day because I was so troubled about my past and my future. I was trying to make something happen that I couldn't make happen. I was doing the same damage I always did, even when I was drunk, because I was the same.

This program gives each and every one of us a way of life. In the forward of the Twelve by Twelve, it says, "A.A.'s Twelve Steps are a group of principles, spiritual in their nature, which, if practiced as a way of life, can expel the obsession to drink and enable the sufferer to become happily and usefully whole" (15). All of my life, I wanted to be happy and usefully whole. The only true happiness I ever had was when I started to have what God says I can because it's permanent. It belongs to me. You can't take it from me. You can't blow your horn at me. You can't call me names. You can't upset me so bad that I become willing to ruin my life over it. You can't do it. It's guaranteed. I can throw it away, but you can't take it from me. I can tell God I don't want you in my life anymore and walk my own way. But this

Twelve Step program makes a difference for each and every one of us.

Many times I'll be working with an alcoholic. He can't find a job, hasn't worked for a year or two. He sends resumes out, but nothing happens. He can't do this, he can't do that. But you put the Steps in his life. Start working with him. He changes. His character changes. All of a sudden he's filling out his resume different. He's talking over the phone different. All of sudden he's got a job again. Because his character has changed, because the disease of alcoholism is being treated, he's new. He's new in every department of his life.

This is about a new way of life for each and every one of us. It's guaranteed. It's guaranteed for you like it's guaranteed for me. But first you have to learn about the disease of alcoholism. It's a hidden disease, and I had to learn how to recognize it. If I have any success, the disease gets hidden. Any money in my pocket, it gets hidden. Any girlfriend, it gets hidden again. Cars, money, any kind of pat on the back, the disease gets hidden.

What happens is my ego comes back. I get strong. I think I'm somebody special again. I think I need special favors, special treatment. I had to learn to be honest about how I think. I had a sponsor that was strong. He had his finger in my nose all the time, telling me, this is the way it is, this is what you have to do, and so on. You have to be honest. I'm not talking about cash-register honesty. I'm talking about self-honesty. How your brain works and how it will control you.

You need total honesty. Total honesty is what is meant by the slogan, "First things first." My sponsor taught me "first things first" right away, before the Steps even. He talked to me about giving my very best shot, in this day, today. I had to learn to do first things first so that when I got going in the Steps, I didn't cut corners, jump ahead, skip this, or skip that. Every day of my life had to be "first things first." Whatever is the major obstacle in your life must be given first consideration. You have to look at it, consider it, not put it aside. Like with me, he put me in the hospital first. Then he paid my hospital bills. After he got me out of the hospital, he got food into my house. He got my wife back, got my job back, paid my bills. He put first things first. He got me started in a productive life because I didn't know how to get started in a productive life myself. All I could do was get sober, hang out in Twelve Step clubs, drink coffee, and suck on Cokes. He knew what to do. He knew how to handle me. He knew how to show me the things I needed to do so that I could have what he had. He told me, "I'm going to show you a way of life where drinking is not necessary. I'm going to take the bumps out of your road." He also said, "This is not a trial-and-error program. I'll give you whatever I have." What my sponsor did is exactly what is meant on page 17 of the Big Book when it says, "The tremendous fact for every one of us is that we have discovered a common solution. We have a way out on which we can absolutely agree, and upon which we can join in brotherly and harmonious action. This is the great news this book carries to those who suffer from alcoholism." Brotherly and harmonious action is what we're doing here now.

What's brotherly and harmonious action? When I got here, I had a brain that was really ratty. I had a brain that was hurting. I hated everything and everybody, and I couldn't do a thing about it because I didn't know what was wrong with me. I would sit in meetings and I would see somebody with a beard. I would say, "I don't like him." He's got a beard, and I figure I don't need a beard. Where I got that from, I have no idea. But I had it. My mind was telling me something, controlling me, and making my life unmanageable. I was restless, irritable, discontented because my mind was not satisfied. My mind was still the power, and I didn't even know why. Finding out who I am is the purpose of finding the Twelve Step program and it's the purpose of Step Two.

Before I could understand who I am, I had to find out about the ABCs of alcoholism. When I talk about the ABCs of alcoholism, I mean alcoholism, ego, and self. The ABCs are about who I am and what's wrong with me. Then, I can go into Steps the way I should instead of the way I did.

I went through the Steps, one at a time, with a sponsor. But when I got through with these Twelve Steps, I was the same as I was before. I was still trying to do the same things I always did. I was still trying to apply these Steps the way I thought they should be applied. I remembered them all, every one of them. I'd go out on a given day and I'd think in terms of Step Two, Step Five, Step Seven, and so on. But I was still trying to make the world the way I wanted it to be, only through the Steps. I missed the point altogether about the power. The power of self. The information about the power of self if being presented right now. You might not need it. Maybe you do, maybe you don't. I need it. After reading this book, you might go out and react to somebody's behavior or to something that happened to you. It clouds your brain and you can't do something you should because you're living backwards and you're living forwards. That's all I ever did. I was a mechanic all my life, and I could go to work blind drunk. I'd be in a blackout, and I'd come to. I'm doing my work, and I don't even know how I got there. But here I am sober now, and I'd be doing the same thing. I'm not blind drunk, but my mind is ten miles away and I'm doing my job. How much of a job can I do that way? My brain was occupied totally by me. That's the disease. What I'm saying is in the Steps.

Now why would they describe the power of self in the Steps? Why would they do that in Step Two? It's the beginning of the program of recovery. I know it's difficult to talk about the Steps. They're so big, so all-encompassing. They cover so much of an area. Can you imagine?

And yet the Twelve by Twelve covers the Twelve Steps in about 105 pages. Step One is covered in four. How could so little material have any effect on your life? What is this message all about? What are we doing here? Why keep coming to meetings after you've been sober for such a long time? Why keep coming? Did you ever stop and ask yourself that question?

I did. The reason I have to continue attending meetings is the same reason I came to meetings in the first place. There's a disease called alcoholism. It's a mind-controlling disease. My brain was hurt a long time ago. It's still hurt today by the power of self, because alcoholism is an "ism." It's never a "wasm." I can't erase it out of my mind. I can't treat it and make it go away. If I'm still living with the same power as I did everything before, it will do everything again the same way. If you don't think so, ask yourself why, in the day you're in, you can't stop doing something you shouldn't be doing. Did you ever find yourself doing something that gave you bad results a hundred times before, and here you are, doing it again, trying to get good results? You're doing the same thing over and over again. You're using the power you used the last time, and that power can only do so much. It can only take you so far. You can't do what you need to do because you're full of your defects of character and your shortcomings.

When I started this program, I knew that meetings were about recovery with a God. I had a program of recovery then, with meetings, readings, and so forth. When I learned about the disease of alcoholism, the Steps became something different. They became something I need. They became an application. They became a way to change character, and a character change is what I need. That's the message for any one of us that has alcoholism.

How much of this recovery do you want? I recognized that there was life to be had here. I wanted every bit of it. I started going for broke. I started doing exactly what is talked about in the Steps, and I started doing it in the day I was in. I had to learn how to keep this message alive, in the moment I was in, no matter what was going down. I had a wife that I loved. She got sick on a Thursday and died on a Sunday morning. In four days, she's dead. I'm looking at her lying there in a casket and wondering what this Twelve Step stuff is all about. Here I am. I come from a rough world. I come from a world where you hurt people. But she never hurt nobody. Now she's dead, and I'm alive. So I wanted to know what this was all about. I couldn't figure it out.

Now I know for sure there is a message here. I know that my God wants me to deliver this message to others. I'm the messenger, not the message. Everything I say or do is already in print. I'll show you exactly where it's at, why it's there, what it's for. This is important to know ahead of time, before you do the Steps. Each one of us has to do the same thing. No matter how much time I have, I have to keep going forward. The reason why is in the Steps. They represent a spiritual life. I have to grow daily, spiritually. The only way I can grow spiritually, daily, is by applying the Twelve Steps. That's the only way any of us can grow. You can pray your life away. You can get up from any prayer and go off and do your own thing. That's what I did for a long time. I thought all I had to do was stay sober and time would heal all things, but time doesn't heal. I can only find healing in the day I'm in, because that's the day my disease needs to be treated. That's the day God is there for me. He gives me all the power that's necessary.

This program of recovery treats alcoholism, and alcoholism has to be treated daily. The disease of alcoholism is always growing, growing all the time. The only difference today is that I don't touch my alcoholism. You might not agree that alcoholism grows, but it's true. The character that I brought here has gotten a lot smarter. The disease that is in my mind, that I used to use, is more capable than it ever was. It's smarter. It can take advantage of situations. It has learned how to lie and not get caught. It has learned how to take advantage of situations so I can get more. That's the disease of alcoholism. It didn't stop when I got sober.

Alcoholism is a mind that I built. I built who I am. No bartenders, no mothers, no fathers, no bosses, nobody else built me. I built me. I found out how to get things, how to push and shove, steal, grab, and take. I found out how to use booze, and as I was using this booze, I was building a character. I was building this character. Nobody else was. This is a tough nut to swallow. At least for me it was. I worked real hard, but I did a lot of damage. I worked harder and still did damage. And then when I got here, I figured all I had to do was stay sober, go to meetings, and things were going to be all right.

The message has to be delivered this way. If the message was not delivered this way, I would never hear it. I would start looking elsewhere. My mind would take over. Once my mind takes over, I want the easier, softer way. I don't want to hear this stuff. I start thinking about how I know too darn much and I've been sober too long. And yet I go out there and keep hurting people. So what am I going to do about this alcoholism? We will go into step application to address this question. But first we will answer some frequently asked questions about the ABCs-Alcoholism, Ego and Self.

▲ You talked a bit about the slogan, "First things first," and how it applies to getting a sponsor and so forth. Could you explain how "First things first" applies to everyday living?

Here is what my sponsor meant when he was talking about "first things first." I should do everything to make my life productive, in the day I'm in. I should look first at the things that are preventing me from living productively in this day. If I don't have a job, I should look for a job instead of sitting at a club, sucking on coffee, and telling everybody how bad my life is. In other words, in the day I'm in, I should do something about getting a job.

Doing first things first would mean putting in an effort,

that day, to do something about my employment. Maybe going to an employment agency, or looking in the newspapers. Every day, there is something that must be attended to, something that must have priority in an effort to make my life manageable.

There are days when I've accomplished a lot and I feel pretty darn good about myself. Maybe I fixed a car when the car needed to be fixed. Maybe I didn't want to work on it, but I did it anyway because I needed the car. Fixing the car was first priority. Whereas, if I had mowed the grass instead, I wouldn't have that car and my life would be unmanageable again. I did not always do things first things first. I would blow things off and my life would become unmanageable again. But I wouldn't live there because it was too full of headaches and too disturbing. So I learned to apply first things first and then I had a manageable life again.

Once you have the application in your life, there will be a time and place for everything. Maybe you got your bills paid, you got a few bucks, you got a job, and your life is in order. Then you are able to start watching TV, or start reading newspapers, or start playing pool, and you'll still have a productive day. You've got a day where there's a place for everything, and you're still in a program of recovery. I find that I now do the things I need to do today without any protest or argument. I do them full steam. I give them everything I've got because first things first is the way it is. First things first is where my happiness is. Life is good, and it gets better all the time.

First things first. This goes with giving 100 percent of yourself. Your life has to be important to you. I don't know about you, but my "living" used to be important to me, my "life" was not important to me. My living was making money, buying things, running here, being satisfied there. That's living. That's not life. Life is about being in the day you're in. It's about looking at a world that you love and seeing the good people in it. It's not about a rat race. I don't want to put myself under that kind of pressure anymore. I don't want to go around kicking myself in the hind end. I don't want to spend my time thinking badly of people all the time. I don't want none of that.

▲ What is it that gets me to finally change my character?

The whole story of the Twelve Step program for all of us, doesn't matter who we are, is the power greater than yourself. This power greater than ourselves is the solution. We've got minds that are hurt. You've got a mind that's bent. Whether you accept that or not I have no idea, but I had to accept it. There's only one thing that will ever change me and that's a power greater than me, and that's God, that's the Lord of my life. Without it, the ego is alive with that old familiar world.

▲ What is God?

It says in Step Two that I came to believe in a power greater than myself that will restore me to sanity. I never had a church, a God, a prayer, a Sunday school, or religious teachings. I had nothing. I didn't believe in nothing. I didn't want to believe in anything. I was a true agnostic. I wasn't an atheist. I was an agnostic. Now I find out that an agnostic is either an ignorant or an uninformed person. And I was both. So page 93 of the Big Book talks about how you can choose any conception of God on three conditions. "If the man be agnostic or atheist, make it empathic that he does not have to agree with your conception of God. He can chose any conception he likes, provided that it makes sense to him. The main thing is that he be willing to believe in a power greater than himself and that he live by spiritual principles." I used to think this was a bunch of bull. And then I hit bottom so hard I wound up in an alkie hospital strapped into a bed that was screwed to the floor. When I got out of there, I was still trying to fight the world. I fought the world for another two-and-a-half years. Now during that fight, I was working and everything else. Things started to get better, but I still knew there was something missing because I had never really changed. My whole life was the same as it was when I was drunk. The bottom line is that I found out I needed something that was better or greater than myself, and the Steps provided a power greater than myself when I applied them. It isn't a question of identifying God as a "what." I know that God is not my brain, but he lies in my brain, in my mind. But God is a power greater than me. Step Two defines this power and Step Three names it. He is the Lord of my life. This is a living power, a living God. He is not a praying god, a god of ritual, a god of yesterday. He is a living God, one who lives in this moment, right now. If I didn't have a living God, what would I have? I'd have me. If I don't talk to God, who do I talk to? Me. You can figure that one out for yourself.

▲ Where does the disease of alcoholism come from?

I was the kind of guy who had to know everything. I had to know about the disease, where it came from, when it was, where it was, why it was and all that. For an alcoholic, those are not important questions. It doesn't make any difference how any of us got like we are. Once alcoholism is established it is understood that the program of recovery is necessary. This is a program of recovery. This is a program of today. This is a program of right now.

▲ Could you elaborate on the concept of the ego factor in alcoholism?

In 1957, *Alcoholics Anonymous Comes of Age* came out. So I got a hold of a copy and read it. The back section, "Medicine Looks at Alcoholics Anonymous," includes a paper written by Dr. Harry M. Tiebout. In 1939, Dr. Tiebout joined AA by proxy. He was AA's first friend in the profession of psychiatry and with whom AA worked in close cooperation. Dr. Tiebout taught about the ego factors in alcoholism.

In the paper, Dr. Tiebout talks about how the ego factors in alcoholism produces grandiosity in the alcoholic. Before I read this paper I never knew anything about the ego factors in alcoholism. I never knew about self and that my mind is distorted by these ego factors. Maybe it's about my appearance, maybe it's about my job. The ego factor is like a value system. I never knew that. When I learned about the ego factor, I began to become aware of the nature of the ABCs of alcoholism. I started to see alcoholism, ego and self, in one person—me. Not looking at myself coming from a drunken world, but actually seeing that I've got something wrong with me. I've got a mind that is injured. It's hurt.

So I found out that alcoholism and ego are in my mind. They are my very being. It's a mind that has a value system. The mind has judgment in it. It thinks you've got something better than me or I should have more than I have because I'm special. I think you should treat me different because I'm a special person. My mind tells me that I do special things and I should be recognized for them, so I try to pat myself on the back for what I do. That's alcoholism thinking. Alcoholism thinking is the allergy that's in me that came from a mental obsession. Even though I'm sober, I'm still carrying the life that I learned to live in the allergy. The mind function that I use comes from a sober mind. I had to recognize, see, become aware of this ego factor in me because of how distorted my mind gets. I use ego for self-satisfaction, for thinking that I am better than you, that I've got more education than you, that I've got a prettier wife than you, or whatever. My brain takes off.

Maybe you criticize me. I'm thin skinned. I want to think I'm real good. I think, "You ain't got the right to talk to me like that." You just got through puncturing my ego and hurting my feelings, and in turn my mind gets real ratty. But my mind doesn't just get ratty when you talk to me.

My mind is always ratty. Lack of power is my dilemma because of alcoholism. Couple up alcoholism with this ego factor and now I am really in trouble. Like when you walk in a room. I used to walk in a room and, right away, I think you are looking at me. When I was drunk I didn't do that, but when I got sober I did. When I'm sober I think you are watching me. I want you to think that I am somebody special. My ego has always got ahold of me, always thinking in terms that I have to prove myself. I have to get your approval and that's ego. That's ego all the time and I don't even know it.

I don't know how to live in the day I'm in as one person to the world, to the whole world, whatever and whoever the world is. Let me tell you, it is a wonderful feeling to be able to have a way of life so that I can be one person to you, to everybody. To not have to wear faces, to not have to play favorites, to not have to play games. I'll tell you, playing favorites is the name of the game for me. I'm always thinking that I only like certain people. If I like you, I'll give you the time of day. I won't pay any attention to the next guy. You can notice it too. When you walk into a room at a big Twelve Step function, meeting, or group, I will say hello to the guy I know, but I won't say hello to a guy that I don't know. He ain't going to do me any good. But there's a buddy over there. I can jive with him. I can have fun with him.

This ego factor is bad stuff. Dr. Tiebout wrote very good articles. You can read his pamphlets for more information. [See bibliography for Dr. Tiebout's pamphlets.] I'll tell you, I have studied Dr. Tiebout and Carl Jung just to find out what the heck is wrong with me, not you, me. I'm always here for me. I'm not here for you. I'm still here for me, even today. I'm not speaking against anybody. I'm not being selfish, because my life depends on this recovery program. I must have it or I won't make it. My life is here. From this program, I can grow and keep growing in a beautiful world that keeps getting better and better. I can admit I'm wrong when I am right. Can you believe that? I mean this, honest to God. I'll take the blame if it'll help you. I mean it. I really mean it. I don't take the blame so you benefit. You might benefit by it, but I don't do it so you benefit. I take the blame so that I benefit. Taking the blame is a hard nut to swallow, especially when the ego factor makes you have to prove a point. This life is so beautiful—without alcoholism and the ego factor. Believe me, it's real.

On Step One

Recovery Begins Now

I admitted I was powerless over alcohol-that my life had become unmanageable.*

Let's open up with the Serenity Prayer.

> God, grant me the serenity to accept the things I cannot change,
> the courage to change the things I can,
> and the wisdom to know the difference.

In the opening chapter, we talked about the ABCs of alcoholism- alcoholism, ego and self. We spoke of the disease of alcoholism and how to recognize it. The ABCs puts the program of recovery into a different light. The steps become a new method for living rather than a method for fixing something and continuing on the way you were before. As I started to learn what was wrong with me, I found that the steps serve a purpose and there is a reason for their numbered order.

Before, I never really knew the purpose of attending meetings, attending meetings and attending meetings, even after you've attended meetings for years. I couldn't get it through my head that life is different every day. Some days

*For the sake of my own recovery, I changed the Steps to first-person singular.

were just spectacular. Some days were awful. But I didn't know that I couldn't use what I used yesterday to live my life today. In life, there are too many variables. Everything changes, and you have to change with it. You have to grow.

The Steps are the same. I must continually apply Steps because things change. Each and every one of us has a life that changes. You don't have a static life. So you can't learn these Steps, graduate, get a diploma, and then you're okay. used to think that the Twelve Steps would modify you and then you would be okay. I didn't know how your character changes when you apply the Steps. I didn't know the purpose of that change.

These Steps are very, very important. This program of recovery is the port of last call. It is a life-and-death proposition. It isn't something you go to school for. It isn't like learning how to add and subtract. The program of recovery is about learning a new way of life so that I can learn how to function today. This is about learning how to live, now, in the day I'm in, so that I'm not out in the world, lost. We talked about the ABCs so that we could have a better chance to realize the purpose of the Steps. Now we will talk about step application.

To put the steps on an individual basis, I had to change the plural pronouns to singular pronouns in the steps. I'll tell you why. After I had gone to a lot of meetings, I started to get too wrapped up in the "we" and "they." I started to think about how I was doing in relationship to the group. I'd start to think that I was way ahead of you or that I knew more than you. So I found that I had to look inward to see what I was doing instead of what everybody else was doing. To do that, I started to change the words to "I" and "me" and "myself."

So I read Step One as "I admitted I'm powerless over alcoho—that my life is unmanageable." Don't get me wrong. I'm not telling you to change the pronouns. I had to because I kept going outside of myself all the time thinking I was smarter, had more years, or went to more meetings than everybody else. Even today I think the same way. Looking inward forces me to focus on what I am doing. Today I'm here for me. I used to be here for everybody else.

I'm living this program of recovery for myself. I'm not doing it for you. I'm really not. Now don't misunderstand that. It's not that I'm not interested in you or that I don't give a darn about you. I'm just saying that I'm doing this for the sake of my own life and my own sobriety. I used to go to meetings, and I'd leave with less than what I brought there. While I was in the meeting, I was in a rat race. I was in my mind, trying to think of what to say. I didn't benefit from the meeting. Somebody could have said something spectacular that I needed to hear and I wouldn't have heard it. I wasn't there. I wasn't paying attention. Later on, when my life was going to pieces, I realized I needed to look at my own life because I couldn't explain my behavior. I was like a rattlesnake. I'd turn on you. Bang! Just like that.

So I have to apply Step One, where I admit that I am powerless over alcohol and that my life is unmanageable. Now in the Big Book, there is no Step One, as far as an application goes. At least to my way of reading those books. Of course, Step One is listed. But as an application, it isn't there. To get to Step One, I have to read "There Is a Solution," "More about Alcoholism," and "We Agnostics." But I can't do that. I just don't have the capability in my mind to understand this Step. How do I admit I'm powerless over alcohol? How is my life unmanageable? What is an unmanageable life? I learned about Step One application from the Twelve by Twelve.

When I admit that I'm powerless over alcohol, I'm admitting that I can never take another drop of alcohol into my body again, for as long as I live. That's a principle. That's a principle I have to use. That's a principle that my new character is being built on, now. This is the principle—that I have the self-honesty to know that I'll never, never be able to take another drink. This is something that I've got to realize. On page 22 of the Twelve by Twelve, Step One introduces how the disease is of a two-fold nature. "The tyrant alcohol wielded a double-edged sword over us; first we were smitten by an insane urge that condemned us to go on drinking, and then by an allergy of the body that insured we would ultimately destroy ourselves in the process." The disease of alcoholism is a mental obsession coupled with a physical allergy. As I mentioned in the ABCs, page 30 in the Big Book says that "the great obsession of every abnormal drinker is that someday he will control and enjoy his drinking." I used to think that I could control my drinking. take it easy. I'd decide not to drink whiskey. I'd just drink beer. But I'd always wind up drunk or even drunker than usual. I found out that the mental obsession, for me, was not just about drinking but about everything. I have a mental obsession. I have a mind that got hurt, that got injured.

I talked a little about this injured mind in the first chapter. I had to create a world that I could live in because I felt the real world was against me. It attacked me. It wasn't satisfying. I wasn't happy. So I learned how to build a character. But I did it through booze. And I figured out how to make sure everything was on my side. I became self-centered. I became a taker. I learned how to do things for my own pleasure and satisfaction. That's the character I brought to the program. That's the character I am, and it's going to stay with me forever.

Now I didn't understand Step One. I thought I could go to a lot of meetings, put in a lot of time, and be successful. I thought the name of the game was staying sober. As the days come and go, you're going to get better because you're sober. Well, my days didn't get better when I first joined this program. In the beginning, things got worse. I did more damage. I never knew the purpose of Step One, so I couldn't benefit from a character change. Now we're talking about a new character, not a modified character. I'm not trying to get rid of little problems here and little problems there and eventually I'm going to be all right. I gotta have a brand-new life. Right at the top of page 63 of *Alcoholics Anonymous*, it says, "As we felt new power flow in, as we enjoyed peace of mind, as we discovered we could face life successfully, as we became conscious of His presence, we began to lose our fear of today, tomorrow, or the hereafter. We were reborn." Being reborn is certainly a good explanation of what happens because, on the same page, there's a Third Step prayer that says, "God, I offer myself to thee—to build with me and to do with me as Thou wilt. Relieve me of the bondage of self …." Look at those words, "the bondage of self." I'm isolated. I'm injured. I'm not very capable of living in the world. I can't love anybody or show them love. I can't have a decent marriage. I can't have a decent friend because I hurt them, injure them, and look at them cockeyed all the time. The Steps say that I can be relieved of the bondage of self and be reborn. The Steps will produce that for me.

So, Step One is not just about stopping drinking. When I admit I'm powerless over alcohol, I am looking at the two-fold nature of the disease. What I'm talking about now is a mental obsession and a physical allergy and I know that either one can kill me. If I don't do something about the mental obsession, it'll kill me. If I don't do something about the physical allergy, it'll kill me. Either way, I'm dead. I had to learn to accept this. I had to accept it because I had so many failures and I wasn't drunk. I had a lot of time in this program and I was still mean and rotten inside. I was upset. I was bad. So that's why Step One has to be introduced in this way. You don't come to this program just to stay sober. You can't just think you'll get the monkey off your back and then you'll do your own thing. You have more to consider, more to identify, so that you don't go through life running into brick walls having bad relationships and bad experiences.

I want to be happy, joyous, and free. Happy, joyous, and free of what? Just from bars and bottles? No way. I want to be happy, joyous, and free from the way my mind controls me and the way I treat people.

Twelve Steps and Twelve Traditions devotes only four pages to Step One. I have to find out why those words are there and what they mean to me because I'm in this program for me. I used to come to this program and live outside of myself. I would look at you, whoever you are, and notice that you had something I didn't have. Maybe you had a prettier wife than I had. Or maybe you had a better car, a better job, more money, better looks. Here's where I had to look at the rest of Step One. I had to realize what an unmanageable life is. I always thought that if you had more money, if you got a better job, if you got the girl and had all the fun, your life would be smooth and nothing would be wrong. But I had to realize just exactly what my life was about. My life isn't about buying new cars or going dancing. That's not what it's about at all. My life is about my mind that evaluates the world, and evaluates me, and then becomes dissatisfied. This is an unmanageable life. My life isn't unmanageable because of one thing. I thought when I got here that I drank too much, that this was what was wrong with me. I was drunk all the time. But it didn't take me long to realize that I was the same sober as I was drunk. I didn't have the drunken behavior, but my life was still unmanageable. Then it started to dawn on me. More and more I accepted the fact that my life was unmanageable whether I was drunk or sober. It doesn't make any difference. I don't need the alcohol in me. I don't need the substance in me. I've got an obsession. I've got a mind that keeps me doing the same things in the same ways without the substance. Without the booze. So I'm getting a little more information about this disease called alcoholism. My life is unmanageable all the time, whether I'm drunk or sober; it doesn't make any difference. That was a hard nut for me to swallow because I was always thinking about satisfying myself. About getting recognized on the job or whatever. But I realized my mind was hurting. My mind was telling me all kinds of things, whether they were true or not. I didn't know how to stop it. I didn't know what the heck was wrong.

As we get further into the Steps, it becomes clearer that I have no control over the life I live. Everything I do, by myself, is always the same. I mean well. But I don't do well. I'm starting to learn that I can't do well because I have a disease. And this disease has a two-fold nature. It's an "ism." It's a mind and body condition. The body condition is the only condition I can treat 100 percent. I can stop drinking. I can stop putting alcohol in me. But what can I do about the obsession? What exactly do I do about that? If I'm the same way drunk as I am sober, that's a death warrant. Whatever I did before, I'll do again. All of my yesterdays are going to be my todays and my tomorrows. Unless I change.

But the good news is that I am in the program of recovery as soon as I start in Step One. I'm in Step One and I'm working really hard. I'm listening at meetings, I've got a sponsor, and I'm writing. I'm doing everything. And I didn't know that this program of recovery is about my life now. Right now. The disease needs to be treated right now.

They explained to me what an unmanageable life is. An unmanageable life is my life, the way I live in the world. There are so many things wrong with my life that have no reference to alcohol. My troubles are not in the bottle anymore. They are in my head, in my mind. The trouble is with the way I act and the way I think. Here I was thinking that all I had to do was mean well and I would do well. No way.

I had to learn by trial and error. Nobody said, "Here's what you do." But the message of this program is found in the Twelve Steps. Without the Twelve Steps, there can't be a message. But there is a message for each and every one of us. Why would any of us come here if we had to suffer and do the same things that we did before? Why can't you be happy, joyous, and free? Why can't you be the new character, in the day you're in? Why can't you be a different person? Why can't you be someone who God wants you to be today?

When I first read Step One, I thought it was something you learned in your head. When I read Step One, I thought I could do something different, but I couldn't do a darn thing different. I didn't know what was wrong, and I still don't know what is wrong. In the Big Book, on page 45, it says,

> Lack of power, that was our dilemma. We had to find a power by which we could live, and it had to be a Power greater than ourselves.

But how was I to find this power? Right now, we're in the application of this step. This is a daily thing. This Step is learning how to do something different than I have before so that I can become a new character. Not a modified character, not a character that means well and can't do well, but a new character. As a new character, I have something going for me that I never had before.

It took me a long time to understand this concept of a new character. When we talk about power in Step Two, we will realize that we are all powers in our own lives. Every one of us is a power. I'm the one who really calls the shots. I'm the captain of the ship. I'm the one who's steering my ship. I had to look at this proposition as life-and-death. This is the port of last call. This program of recovery is prime time. It can be no better than this new way of life because my life is at stake.

What I'm talking about is already in print. It's already established what to do, how to do it, and with whom to do it. My mind is still closed. It has always been closed, but at least now I'm becoming aware of something. Before, I was blind. I was blind as a bat. And I couldn't hear either. I didn't want to hear. I can't stop behaving like a jerk because I'm macho. I think I'm strong. I think I can take care of everything. I'm afraid to tell you, whoever you are, I don't know what the heck I'm doing. I'm sick. I'm sick in the stomach. Not physically sick. Sick in behavior. I'm sick in my life. I'm sick in everything I think, even sober, because I'm walking around kicking myself in the hind end all the time. I don't know the disease of alcoholism. I don't know what the disease is but it's coming more and more to the surface. So I learn to look at it, not to do anything about it, but just to look at it. You might be able to go farther than I did. I couldn't because I had to do everything my way. Right away, I look at you, whoever you are, and I don't like you. Because I don't know the disease of alcoholism.

As we get into the Steps a little more, we'll talk about what to do. This "little more" means a great deal to me because we'll be talking about building a new character. As a sponsor, I know for sure that I can't tell you, "Here's Step One, let's read it and now we'll go on to Step Two ...." That would be signing a death warrant for you. Rather, we will go into the Steps as an application for a way of life.

But first lets answer some frequently asked questions on Step One.

▲ Something is not clear to me. When I apply the Steps, do I completely change my character or do I remain the same person?

The first thing to understand is the Twelve Steps are a group of principles. As I mentioned before, on page 15 of the *Twelve Steps and Twelve Traditions*, the Twelve Steps "are a group of principles, spiritual in their nature, which, if practiced as a way of life, can expel the obsession to drink and enable the sufferer to become happily and usefully whole." The main thing I have to recognize is that this program doesn't modify me. It doesn't give me something extra so that I can keep what I got, what brought me here. It doesn't do that. It can't do that. It's impossible. I came here because there is something wrong with the character that I am already. I built this character. I learned to live in the world by fighting, by grabbing, by taking, by pushing, and by shoving. Well, I didn't know that I was building a character out there. That character is my mind. It's me. That's who I am. I can't do anything except what I've been doing and this is what I can't accept. My head tells me that I can do something now, sober, and get away with it. But I can't. I don't have the capacity to do what needs to be done. I'm always influenced by my own selfishness, my own self-satisfaction. That's what page 60 in the Big Book is about when it says, "The first requirement is that we be convinced that any life run on self-will can hardly be a success. On that basis we are almost always in collision with something or somebody, even though our motives are good."

To have a change of character, I first have to identify the old character. That's what Steps One to Six are all about. Steps One to Six are about the disease of alcoholism and about me. Not about somebody else. And so Steps One to Six tell us we have to look at ourselves as alcoholics to see what's wrong with us and see who we are. When it says in there that I admit that I'm powerless over alcohol and that my life is unmanageable, that's me. That's not you. That's me. This book was written for me. I'm the one that's hurting. I'm the one that's in trouble. I'm the one that does damage. So let's put this in the right perspective. I am building a new character. In the process, I must look at the old character.

▲ What are the principles that come out of Step One?

The main principle is that I'll never be able to take another drop of alcohol into my body for the rest of my life. That's the main principle. That's number one. That's the purpose of Step One. When I admit that I'm powerless over alcohol, that's the story of Step One. I'll never be able to have success drinking again. This principle is not talked about. If you're working with a baby, and he goes out and gets drunk, I have to tell you that he got drunk because he didn't get some information that he needed. He didn't get Step One. He thought he could do something again and get away with it. He—or she—didn't know any better. Their mind told them, "I can handle this now. I know what to do now. Now that I've gone to some meetings, I'm okay. I know what the trouble is. I know where it's at." They never did know anything. They didn't do what was necessary.

Character building has to start with Step One. Where else would it start? Step One says that I'm powerless over alcohol. Now I'm not going to accept that. You're going to have to show me that. You'll have to tell me that, and you'll have to help me understand that. In the Big Book, it talks about how we don't have good memory. We can't remember a week ago, a month ago, or whatever our last drunk did to us. We can't remember how we hurt people and how we acted. We don't recall it, so what do we do? You think, "Well, I'll be okay this time. I won't behave that way." So we pick up the bottle and drink again. That's the disease of alcoholism.

I don't believe that recovery "takes what it takes." I don't believe you have to hang around for five years or you have to suffer so many years before you can have recovery. That's not right. It can't be right. What kind of God would do that to us? Is that the kind of God this program is talking about? A God who does for me what I can't do for myself? No way. Recovery is now. This is serious business. This is life and death. And I mean it's life and death now. I've had babies who took their own lives because this information wasn't presented to them. So the main principle of Step One is that I can never take another drink for as long as I live.

▲ You talk about awareness. What are we becoming aware of?

I like to use the word "awareness" more than the word "understanding." To me, understanding is head knowledge, an opinion up here in my head. That's all it is. I need to identify something as it really is, not as I think it is. To me, that's awareness. I need to become aware of my behavior. I need to be alert. Before, my head would tell me, "I understand. I understand everything. I know a great deal. I've been around for a long time." And then I would turn around and do the same darn thing that got me into trouble before. See, my head told me, "You're smart. You're all right." So "understanding" is a bad word in my vocabulary. I try not to use it. I bite my tongue when I say it. I may have understood everything, but I wasn't aware of anything. No way. I would go out and act like a fool, just like I always did. Look at your own track record. How many times did you get into a beef with somebody, and the argument didn't have anything to do with your life?

Today I'm aware that I am argumentative. So I know I'm going to back down. I can, too, because backing down is about saving my life. Even if you think less of me, I don't care. When I back down, my life is better. I don't have to ruin my mind, my life, or my friendships. What you've asked is very important. This program is a never-ending story in application.

▲ In the application of Step One, am I accepting my old character as it is or am I trying to be a new character? Second, how can I do either of these things if I haven't begun to apply Step Two?

These are valid questions. When you come to the program, you don't go through all Twelve Steps before you start treating the disease. That's wrong. That's all wrong. If it worked that way, you'd never make it. I wouldn't make it either. The program of recovery is in a logical order and so the Steps are numbered in order One through Twelve. You start building your new character not when you come to the program but when you begin to apply the Twelve Steps in your daily life. If it was a question of having to get through so many steps before you could have your disease treated, we wouldn't make it. None of us would. You can't go out into the world and have any success at all without having your obsession at least identified and recognized. You can't do it. I've known too many alcoholics that come to the program, stay sober for some time, and then say, "I'm sober but I don't know why." I knew exactly what happened to me, what I was, and why I wound up where I did. I knew it was from alcohol and I knew darn well there was no way I could stay sober by myself. Before this program, I tried on too many days, in too many ways, to not drink, and I couldn't do it. As soon as I begin in Step application, I am building a new character. This character can stop drinking. But to do so I must accept my alcoholism. On page 21 of the Twelve by Twelve it says, "We know that little good can come to any alcoholic who joins A.A. unless he has first accepted his devastating weakness and all its consequences. Until he so humbles himself, his sobriety—if any—will be precarious. Of real happiness he will find none at all."

To apply Step One you do not need Step Two to build the new character. To apply Step One all I need to do is accept that I can never drink again and that I have a warped mind that creates an unmanageable life, drunk, sober and forever if left untreated. The purpose of the Steps is to treat this disease by building a new character without any reference to the old character.

None of us can be the old character and the new character together. None of us can. You might not recognize that, but it's true for me. There's no way I could be a little bit of this and a little bit of that. No way I can do it that way. I can't have the disease and have God, too. It doesn't work. It just won't work. You have to recognize exactly what these Steps are doing, why they're doing it, and how they're doing it. That's what the ABCs were about. In Step One, it says that my life's unmanageable. By applying Step One, you have begun to build this new character. Then you go on to Step Two. And that's where we're going now.

Part 2

Surrender: The Ending of the Old Life and the Beginning of the New Life

On Step Two

Keeping an Open Mind

Came to believe that a power greater than myself could restore me to sanity.*

Step Two reads: "Came to believe that a power greater than myself could restore me to sanity." The first thing about this Step that I had to learn is that there is a power greater than myself.

One of the first requirements to find this power greater than self is that you have to have an open mind. On page 26 of the Twelve by Twelve it says, "First, Alcoholics Anonymous does not demand that you believe anything. Second, to get sober and stay sober, you don't have to swallow all of Step Two right now. Third, all you really need is a truly open mind. Just resign yourself from the debating society and quit bothering yourself with such deep questions as whether it was the hen or egg that came first." Now I never knew what an open mind was. I just didn't get the drift of this at all. I'm a strong person, with a powerful mind that tells me what to do and I think it's okay. So I didn't think I needed to look at myself.

But this Step is talking about another kind of power, a

*For the sake of my own recovery, I changed the Steps to first-person singular.

power that operates in the day I'm in, no matter what my mind is thinking and no matter what I'm feeling. I have to identify what this power is, if there is such a power. Is it greater than me? Why is it greater than me? What does it mean that I have to believe or come to believe in a power greater than me?

I had great problems with this concept because I don't know how to define God. I don't talk to God. I don't pray to God. I don't even want to. I don't even want you to tell me about it. I don't want to hear it. I don't want to be around it. That's the way I was. That's the character I was when I got here. And so, to believe in something, I had to be taught.

Another alcoholic told me what he did with this Step, and he suggested that I try that. And I did. At work, I started to identify something other than myself operating in my life. So I started to think in terms of actually talking to something other than myself. To come to believe in something, I can't just say I believe in it. I have to be taught what to do. Everything happens really fast in my world. My action and reaction are instantaneous. I haven't got time to think, "Do I need God? Should I pray here? Should I pray there? What is it I should do?" Things happen too fast.

I didn't know that my character had to change. I had to change completely so that I could act differently, without any reference to the way I used to act. I had to learn that I couldn't use my old character. I had to be reborn, as it says on page 63 of the Big Book. I can't be in this program, thinking alcoholic thoughts one minute and recovery thoughts the next minute. I can't do it.

Character is built through principles. You start with Step One with the principle of staying sober, meaning that I can't drink again and that my life is unmanageable when I'm on my own, whether I'm drunk or sober. Then I come to Step Two where I have to learn to believe in something other than me so that I can talk to something other than myself. How can I believe in something greater than myself if I stay with myself?

I can't do it. It's impossible. I accepted this power mentioned in Step Two because there was no "God" mentioned there and no "higher power." That application comes later. All it says is that I came to believe in a "power greater than myself." Those words enable me to listen to you. So I don't block what you're saying. I'll at least let you present it to me. To believe in this kind of power, I have to associate my life with something, maybe the program, and agree that there is something in this world besides myself.

Now the word "sanity" has to be explained. The program defines sanity as soundness and wholeness of mind on page 33 of the Twelve by Twelve. I knew exactly what this meant because my life was in a mess. In a turmoil. Here I was sober, but I was fighting mad. I was upset. I drove my car a hundred miles an hour. I do everything fast and furious, mean and mad. My life is crazy. It's nuts. I don't have soundness or wholeness of mind. I have a mind that's injured. I have a mind that's scattered.

For me to want to be different, I have to act different. I started talking to a power that was greater than me. I started identifying the fact that I need help. Now there's no way I got down on my knees. I didn't do that until Step Three. And I didn't pray from a position of knowing God or even of trying to know who he is. I just prayed and asked something to help me with my hostility and anger, hoping something would happen. I couldn't go any farther. I didn't want to go any farther than that. I was against everything. I was against God. I was against your God. I was against your talk, your beliefs, your everything. But to come to believe in a power greater than myself meant that I had to do something different.

Now I didn't get the requirement about having an open mind. I didn't know what they meant by an "open mind." So I tried to figure out what a closed mind was. I had a closed mind. I knew that, so I knew they were talking about me. But I didn't really know the difference between a closed mind and open mind. Later I found out that a closed mind is occupied by self, and only by self. If you have an open mind, it doesn't mean that self isn't there. An open mind is not a mind that's stupid, dumb, or uneducated, or anything like that. It's a mind that does not have any preconceived ideas. An open mind is exactly that: open, receptive. I can put something in there. I can look at something in different ways. I had to learn what an open mind was in all my affairs, not just at meetings. Not just when I was in trouble. Not just when I was mad. I have to have an open mind for everything. *Everything*.

This was real, real difficult for me because it meant I had to start backing down. I had to bite my tongue. I had to turn and walk away from it. I get so mean and mad, I'll try to destroy something. Now I had to learn to back down and not destroy it. Backing down was a start. By the way, backing down is what set me free to follow the purpose of the Twelve Steps. I would never have been able to have Step Three in my life if Step Two hadn't been presented clearly enough for me to recognize the power and to use it. Now I can do this step. I can actually do it. Today, this day. Maybe you think you know what Step Two is, but I didn't know. Right now, on this day right here, can you have an open mind? Is your mind really open right now? Can you listen and look at something and hold out the possibility that an idea is maybe right, maybe wrong? Can you approach everything you do in that manner? Can you look at other people and accept what they say the way it's said and not want to change it? Or do you want to tell them they are wrong, that "this is crazy" or that "this would never work"? You should ask yourself these questions. If you're an alcoholic, you're going to have to do this until the day you die. If your mind slams shut, you're going to be stuck with your old self and your past. You're going to relive and redo every mistake you ever made. You're going to hurt people. An open mind is a must to go further into the Steps. In Step Three, there is a requirement to do something and you can't do it until you have an open mind.

What I am describing is a program of recovery, an

application of steps, of principles, of truths. This application is about changing my character. I am becoming a new character. I'm backed up by principles with no reference to yesterday's life or my old character. No reference. I have to clear away the wreckage of the past. This new character doesn't need to remember how the old person acted or what he did. The program of recovery is a brand-new life.

As I quoted before, page 85 of *Alcoholics Anonymous*,says: "We are not cured of alcoholism. What we really have is a daily reprieve contingent upon the maintenance of our spiritual condition." We're starting right now to get into spiritual condition. What I am saying is true. The open mind must be there all the time, today, right now. The argument against anything has to stop. Living in the world with a dissatisfied mind has to stop. It's got to stop. I'm sober and I'm trying to make a new life, a new character. I'm trying to do the will of God. Step Two qualifies me to go on and do Step Three. In Step One, I started building a new character in principle. Step One needs Step Two to continue to build this new character. You can't do one Step and go on and forget that Step, that application, that truth. You can't do it.

We don't have a choice in this program of recovery. We can't decide when to do something or when not to do it. I lost the power of choice, not just in drinking, but in thinking and in living. I lost the ability to think to good purpose. That is what is meant on page 45 of the Big Book when it says, "Lack of Power" is my dilemma. I cannot choose to apply the program of recovery. I must have it. Otherwise self would be in the picture. This is about how to think and act to good purpose. This is about being able to live in the day you're in, without the quarrel and without a closed mind. An open mind, believe me, is really important. All of my life, I've been programmed to think one way, to do one way, to figure there's only one way to do something. An open mind will set me free, even if I don't know it. I need to have an open mind just to have a decent relationship with another human being.

At the end of its discussion of Step Two, the Twelve by Twelve says, "Some will be willing to term themselves 'problem drinkers,' but cannot endure the suggestion that in fact they are mentally ill." In the chapter on Step One, it says, "It is truly awful to admit that, glass in hand, we have warped our minds ...." I have to realize that what the literature is talking about is the disease of alcoholism. I have a warped mind. I am mentally ill. So I have to start now and build a new character with no reference to the old character. None at all.

Here are some questions related to this step:

▲ What do you do when you believe you're the power? Suppose you think that if you don't do it, it won't get done right. Or you figure, it's your way or the highway. That sort of thing. How do you get from there to the other kind of power?

That's the purpose of what we are doing now—to learn about self and to learn about a power greater than self, so that I do not have to repeat me. If I believe in a power greater than myself, I stand a chance. This is about a relationship. You have to believe in, not pray to, a power greater than yourself. Now to do that, you have to learn how to back down. And you have to learn to recognize when you're up to your old tricks. I've caught myself and found myself saying, "I'm sorry, God. I'm up to my old tricks. Forgive me. I'm at it again." There is a way for each and every one of us to stop doing what we shouldn't do. As you begin to apply the other Steps, your relationship to this power greater than self gets stronger. So when I am using my power it becomes very obvious. I call these "The Ominous Signs." When I show resentment, fear, anger, hostility or when I look at the world and question it, pick on it, find fault with it, it becomes obvious that's the power of self.

▲ But if you think it's your way or no way at all?

Again, it's the same thing as trying to play God. It would be better to answer your question in Step Seven because that's where this issue comes up the most. When my self is in the picture, I'm restless, irritable, discontented. I can't be like that anymore. This is a program of recovery. As it says on page 58 of *Alcoholics Anonymous*, "If you have decided you want what we have and are willing to go to any lengths to get it—then you are ready to take certain steps." If you really want to recover, in the day you're in, you are going to get less and less into the power of self.

The disease must be treated now, in the life that you lead today. You can't treat it in the life you led yesterday or the life you are going to lead tomorrow. That's impossible. Now, you have to look at when the disease gets treated. Right now. Are you receptive, right now, to do the things that need to be done and to want to lead a good life? This program of recovery has to operate always in the present moment. I don't know if you believe that or not. Maybe you can't hear it, but I'll keep telling it to you. That's because the disease is treated right now and the way it is for me, right now. I could forget when the disease gets treated—at any time. I could stop reading. I could stop applying the Steps. I could go ahead, in the day I'm in, and think to myself that there's nothing wrong with my life and that there's nothing I have to do today to make it better. You and I need God in our lives. I need a power greater than me in my life, whether what's going down is good or bad. Otherwise, I have another power in my life, the power of self, that takes over. It's an aberrant mind. It's a mind that's bent, warped. This is a mind that's going to repeat the same things over and over again, even if they've never worked.

How do I stop myself? The truth is: I can't stop it. But a power greater than me can. The step says I came to believe in a power greater than myself that could restore me to sanity.

Now if I could restore myself to sanity, I wouldn't even need the program of recovery. I would not need to spend over forty-four years of my life applying the program of recovery. My own track record proves that I can't do it on my own. No matter whether I'm drunk or sober. I need a power greater than myself to do for me what I can't do myself. All of us need this power greater than ourselves.

▲ Please repeat your definition of the open mind and the closed mind.

An open mind is something I never could understand. At first, I just wouldn't buy it. I didn't think it was anything but words. But I've got to understand that an open mind is something that operates without reference to self. The self isn't there, telling me to do things and showing me how to act. An open mind helps me learn what's going on in my daily life.

An open mind doesn't help me with just one thing either. It helps me with everything. An open mind is a receptive mind that self doesn't occupy. It's a mind empty of self. Not just one thing, either, but everything. If I'm arguing against something, wanting something, not accepting something, finding fault with something, looking out at the world and trying to change it, my mind is closed. Maybe it's too hot or too cold; maybe the freeway is too full; whatever it is I'm arguing with it. That's an argumentative mind. That's a closed mind that is talking to me and giving me information that upsets me. This is a mind that Dr. Silkworth, in the Big Book on page xxvi, calls "restless, irritable, and discontented." My life is restless, irritable, and discontented because I'm arguing and fighting all the time. I'm looking at the world, moaning and groaning, not knowing that the mind is closed.

▲ What is a good example of alcoholic insanity?

Alcoholic insanity is exactly what I was talking about before. If I think I can get away with doing something that has never worked before, that's alcoholic insanity. I'm going to make this thing fit no matter how ridiculous it is. I'm going to continue on, doing the same things I've done before, even though they've never worked.

The thing that stopped me in Step Two was that I didn't think I was insane. In fact, I knew I wasn't. So I had trouble with the idea of being "restored to sanity." But the step isn't talking about doing things that are so extreme or so far from the norm that you have to be institutionalized. We might get into that with some of our behavior, but that's not insanity. When the Step talks about being restored to sanity, it's talking about being restored to soundness of mind, a wholeness of mind, a wellness of mind. A sound mind is an open mind. Suppose you're reading this chapter and you're having trouble staying on track. Maybe you're bored or maybe something I've said bothers you. But you stay with it. That's soundness of mind. That's self-discipline. Self-discipline is something you need in every aspect of your life as an alcoholic with alcoholism. You're learning self-discipline right now, but you'll learn more by applying these Steps than by reading these words.

What we're talking about here is having an open mind. The open mind will give me sanity, soundness of mind, wholeness of mind, wellness of mind, because there will be something besides my self occupying me. That is the program of recovery. That is the power greater than me. It can do what I can't do. And it's not even named yet. That'll come in the next Step.

▲ How much, if any, credit do you take for the recovery of someone you sponsor?

A long time ago, I had a real problem with taking credit. It had to be a problem so that I could find out who I really was. I used to think I was responsible for your life. I thought that I could make you sober and make you do things. I thought that if I crammed this program of recovery down your throat hard enough, you would get it. As far as taking credit for someone else's recovery, sure I did it. I used to put guys in hotels, pay their bills, let them stay there for a week, and then I'd go around and talk about it. I'll be talking more about taking credit as we get more into the Steps. There isn't one of us who can do anything, in the day we're in, without the grace of God upon us. Not one of us.

▲ So does Step Two come down to simply having an open mind?

No way. No. But an open mind is a requirement. In other words, if you're reading this book with a closed mind, you might as well go out and go to the beach. Or do anything else. That's the truth.

▲ The last paragraph on Step Two in the Twelve by Twelve reads, "True humility and an open mind can lead us to faith." And on page 58, it says that humility "amounts to a clear recognition of what and who we really are, followed by a sincere attempt to become what we could be." Also, Step Seven defines humility as "a desire to know and do God's will." In an application of Step Two, how do you define humility?

Humility isn't in Step Two, in the sense that they're talking about there. You're building a character in this program. You're building it by application of the Steps. And starting with Step One, the Steps are in a specific order. Humility is not a quality that's needed at this point. You can't jam the whole program into someone all at once. That's why the Steps are in a logical order. Step Two is there so that you can do Step Three. And Step Three, which is the foundation of the program, is all about God. When you get to Step Seven, which is possible only by the application of the preceding Steps, you can have humility and humbleness. At that point, humility is something you're qualified to have. In other words, you can't come to this program, apply Step One, and think you've got the whole package. You can't just walk into meetings and be happy, joyous, and free. There's no way. You have to build a new character. But as you're building that character, you're growing spiritually and you're building a life with principles through the application of the Steps.

Like I've said several times, the Steps are in the order they are in for a reason. You'll note that Steps One through Six are about the disease. Those Steps are about the old character. Those Steps are an explanation of what's wrong, what's needed, and what you have to do to build a new character. But when you go to Steps Seven through Twelve, you're talking about something different. We're taking the character from Steps One through Six into Step Seven. After Step Seven, it's possible to look outward more instead of inward and to stop wondering "what's in it for me" and "what will I get out of it" all the time. On page 70 of the Twelve by Twelve, it says that alcoholics must "develop much more of this precious quality than may be required just for sobriety" or "they still haven't much chance of becoming truly happy." When adversity comes, you won't know what to do if you don't have humility. You've got to have much more going for you than just being sober.

▲ Many times you mentioned the phrase, "an alcoholic with alcoholism." Is there such a thing as an alcoholic without alcoholism?

Sure there is. You bet. If you come to this program just to

get sober but to remain who you are, if you treat the alcoholic when he's drunk but don't change the rest of his life, if you do nothing else but attend meetings to stay sober, you're talking about alcoholics without alcoholism. In this program of recovery, each individual identifies alcoholism as a disease of the mind. The alcoholic without alcoholism doesn't identify with the disease. He just wants to stay sober. He can be sober and be the most miserable person in the world, but that's his business. That's not my business. When you say you're an alcoholic with alcoholism, you cross over an invisible line. You're in a world where you admit you can never behave any differently by yourself. Alcoholism is a disease. Each one of us has to recognize alcoholism as a disease in ourselves. Sure there's a big difference between an alcoholic and a heavy drinker. There's a big difference between an alcoholic and a drinker who doesn't give a darn about his life. His life is not important. But when he has alcoholism, believe me, he's facing a life-and-death proposition.

▲ You have said, "I am here for me." How does this relate to carrying the message to others?

When I first came to this program, I thought the name of the game was staying sober, picking up babies, and getting them to meetings. And that's what I did. I couldn't get them in my car, there were so many. There weren't many meetings then. Heck, there were only five meetings in the whole San Fernando Valley. And the San Fernando Valley is a big place. They had meetings in Reseda, San Fernando, North Hollywood, Burbank, and Glendale. That's all. No place else. If you wanted to go to other meetings, you had to go over in Los Angeles some place. But in those days, when my disease wasn't being treated, you didn't really want to be helped by me. I'd just show you how to get meaner and madder. I'd teach you how to tear somebody apart better than you already knew how to do it. So I had to become the new character before I could help people.

This new character is about attraction, not promotion. It's attraction. I learned about attraction from my sponsor. He was a quiet man who helped people and gave them his life. He gave people money, time, opportunities. He was who he said he was. But to be someone like that, he had to do something.

Now I would go to meetings and I'd hear some guy talking. I'd listen to him, and I'd know all he was talking about was crap. He was talking about harm. He's moaning. I'd listen to another guy and he's talking about the good life. He's talking about happiness. He's talking about having success in his life, today: vacations, fishing, paying bills, stuff that belongs to him. He's recognizing the day he is in and talking about it. Me, I'm talking about yesterday. The first guy was talking about yesterday. I don't want to be like him. I want to be like the guy who's talking about the good life, today. Attraction is what it is all about. How can you help somebody if you haven't changed? On page 64 of Alcoholics Anonymous, it says, "Obviously you cannot transmit something you haven't got." And that's the truth. This is a hard nut to swallow. It really is, but I don't want to fight the world anymore. I don't want to walk in the room, looking at people, hating them, judging them, criticizing them, wondering what the heck is the matter with them. That's baloney. It's about my life, who I am. I need to be the new character before I can carry this message. Now you can see why Step 12 is in the twelfth position.

On Step Three

Where Willpower Comes In!

Made a decision to turn my will and my life over to God as I understood Him.*

If I go into Step Three without applying Steps One and Two first, I won't be able to make a decision to turn my will and my life over to the care of God as I understood him. I'll take the decision back.

When you make a decision, you're either deciding to do something or not to do something. In this Step, the decision is specific. It says that "I made a decision to turn my will and my life over to the care of God as I understood Him." That means I have to make a decision to do something. To be able to do this thing, I have to figure out what this Step means by turning my will and my life over to the care of God. I have to figure it out. I have to talk about it. I have to recognize what the Step means by "my will and my life." What is my will and my life? I had to learn that my "will" is my very being. My will is my mind. My will is the way I am. Consciously and unconsciously, I am this character. My will is my true character. I am that character, and I'm going to have to do something with it now.

*For the sake of my own recovery, I changed the Steps to first-person singular.

Now remember that Step Two has taught me how to build a relationship. Step Three, by definition, has to teach me how to do something else. It's going to teach me that I have to turn my will and my life over to the care of God. And this Step is starting to talk about a God "as I understood Him." It doesn't say "understand Him." It says "understood Him." "Understood" is referring to the power that was introduced in Step Two. This power is going to restore me to sanity. But now Step Three is naming the power. The power has to be named because I am making a decision to go to this power. Not to go to the power of me but to go to the power who is greater than me, which is God. It says so in Step Three. As I *understood* him.

When we refer to God "as I understood Him," we don't mean we understand God. The meaning of "understood" has to be clarified. I had to hear the meaning of "understood" more than once. I had to realize it more than once, and I had to keep it alive. Try to stay open to what I'm saying now. Don't file it away in your file cabinet, like I used to do. The principle is that I must be with a power greater than myself. That's a truth. We started to build a character down in Step One by applying principles and truths. Just learning these Steps is worthless, worthless, because you'll hear them and just file them away and do your own thing. Your own thing is whatever the power of self tells you to do. I didn't know that I can actually be somebody different today because of the power of Step Three. Step Three is the foundation for each and every one of us because of what you have to do.

I have to turn my will and my life over to the care of God *as I understood him*. My life is right now. Where I am, whatever I'm doing right now, that's my life. My will is something else. It's my intelligence, my memory, my file cabinet, my yesterdays, my tomorrows. So I have to turn my will over to the care of God as I understood him. With Step Two, which taught me to have an open mind, I can now do something. I can now make a decision to do something different than before. I don't have to keep modifying this decision. I can just make it. I can put my will and my life into the care of a power, which is called God and which can do something I can't do.

There are two powers now. I know there are two powers. There's one world, but there are two concepts for this world. My power and God's power. That's what I'm going to have to look at now. My world is the world I brought here from my drunken world, and it's the same world when I'm sober. It's no different. No different. And that's proven. But there's another world. God's world. God's world is the world I want to live in. It's the world that they've promised me in the literature. In the Twelve by Twelve on page 35 it says,

> To every worldly and practical-minded beginner, this Step looks hard, even impossible. Now matter how much one wishes to try, exactly how can he turn his own will and his own life over to the care of whatever God he thinks there is? Fortunately, we who have tried it, and with equal misgivings, can testify that anyone, anyone at all, can begin to do it. We can further add that a beginning, even the smallest, is all that is needed. Once we have placed the key of willingness in the lock and have the door ever so slightly open, we find that we can always open it some more. Though self-will may slam it shut, as it frequently does, it will always respond the moment we again pick up the key of willingness.

These words fit my vocabulary, my mind, because they are action words. They are words with which I associate my life. One of the words that's important to me has just been used: "willingness." The other word I had to learn was "open-mindedness." These are words that are important to me. I keep using them in the day I'm in so that I can keep an open mind. These words are not words now. These words are my life. My life is governed by this word: "willingness." Willingness doesn't mean you just pray to God or have God in your life. Willingness is about building a character that doesn't argue. He doesn't fight. He doesn't have opinions. He doesn't have a file cabinet full of material that he shouldn't use. Willingness is a character-building principle. Willingness is a principle.

Now willingness is for everything. Everything. If you have soundness of mind, you, as an alcoholic with alcoholism, will not have a distorted view and you won't go after things you shouldn't. Soundness of mind says "no" and willingness says, "I gotta go for something good this time. I'm not going to do that again." Willingness is wanting and needing what you should have. All these words are important. To me they are. This is a vocabulary. This is *the language of the heart*.

Other words from the program play a big role in my life. Words like "surrender" and "acceptance." All of these words are a part of my life. These words are in my brain, my mind. I must have this stuff. This "stuff" I'm talking about isn't mine. It's in print. These principles are proven. They are like mathematical principles, just like two plus two equals four. You can't change that equation. Look at the literature. Page 27 of the Twelve by Twelve tells you "the basic principle of scientific progress: search and research, again and again, always with the open mind." You can't have a principle just by hearing it, looking at it, reading it. You have to apply it, use it, be it. Character must be backed up by principles. That's why I can do things today that I couldn't do before. My character is backed up by principles that give me a constant, consistent life that is good. And it keeps getting better. Now I don't turn all of a sudden and go in a different direction. I don't, all of a sudden, say, "I'd better lie to get myself out of trouble." That would make me a liar again, and I don't want to go in that direction.

The basis of my life is a power greater than myself. God. Now this relationship allows me to face life. I can stand on my own two feet. I can look you in the eye and tell you something. I don't have to remember how to tell my story today because I lied to you yesterday.

I'm talking about me now. I'm not preaching, believe me. But I'm telling you something I learned to do, and to keep doing, only by the grace of God and the Twelve Steps of this program. This is why I came to this program and why I keep coming to meetings. It's not like it used to be for me, a big popularity contest, where you get up to speak, and get big pats on the back, and everything like that. No, it's not like that now for me. This 12-Step program is my life. Without this program, I will die. I will have to get drunk, go insane, or do something to destroy myself.

Step Three is the foundation that enables each one of us, as an alcoholic with alcoholism, to do something. Now what do you do? You turn your will and your life over to God's care, as it's understood. It's understood now, from Step Two, that we're all doing the same thing. This foundation is the solution, right now, that everybody talks about. "We have a way out on which we can absolutely agree, and upon which we can join in brotherly and harmonious action" (*Alcoholics Anonymous* 17). If you're an alcoholic with alcoholism, you need what I need. You can't add anything to or take anything away from the Twelve Steps and make them any stronger, quicker, or better. They are in their entirety, all the way. The steps are a closed circuit. If you stay in the Twelve Steps, you find the life you've always wanted and your disease will be treated.

There's a lot to Step Three. In the Twelve by Twelve on page 40 it says:

> Then it is explained that other Steps of the A.A. program can be practiced with success only when Step Three is given a determined and persistent trial. This statement may surprise newcomers who have experienced nothing but constant deflation and a growing conviction that human will is of no value whatever.

I always thought a newcomer was somebody who just came into the program off the street, somebody who was drunk, or somebody who had never heard of the program. Now I know that I'm a newcomer, in the day I'm in, when I'm lost, when I don't know what to do, when I've been around for years and I'm still up to my old tricks. I no longer think of the newcomer as being you because you're drunk or you just got here. Now I know that the newcomer is me and that it has to be me for me to grow spiritually. What I'm saying is important. It goes on to say in the Twelve by Twelve on page 40:

> They had become persuaded, and rightly so, that many problems besides alcohol will not yield to a headlong assault powered by the individual alone. But now it appears that there are certain things which only the individual can do. All by himself, and in the light of his own circumstances, he needs to develop the quality of willingness. When he acquires willingness, he is the only one who can make the decision to exert himself. Trying to do this is an act of his own will. All of the Twelve Steps require sustained and personal exertion to conform to their principles and so, we trust, to God's will.

The reason I quote this is because of the line, "When he acquires willingness, he is the only one who can make the decision to exert himself." For a long time, I did not know this program was about me, myself, the way I act, the way I behave, how much I read, how much I believe, how much I pray, and how much I go to meetings. These are about acts of my own will.

My own will is a power, and my own will would rather sit somewhere and watch TV. My own will says I don't need to do this. I'm all right. I've done that, and I'm okay. If I don't make a decision to turn my will and my life over to the care of God, I'm going to start using my own will again.

What's going on here? Are we trying to fix things? I used to think that if you got certain things fixed, you could go ahead and live your life. No way. You can't do it. So what's going on here is that I'm trying to learn how to have something in my life that I've never had before. I have to turn my will and my life over to the care of God *as I understood him*. I can't use the power that's me. I have to use the other power, which is God.

When I make a decision, what's that mean? What's a decision? A decision is a daily function, a daily thing. When I become willing, what does that mean? What's willingness about? It's about the mind that I use. I become a willing character. I want to do everything, in the day I'm in, the best I can. So my will starts to come into alignment with God's will. I can use my will, now, in the way it should be used. This step is the foundation that allows you and me, as alcoholics with alcoholism, to live in the day we're in. We don't have to be confronted with our own limited brains, our minds that say it should be this way and not that way. Now I've got an open mind. Step Two has prepared me to find out what they want me to find in Step Three.

When I turn my will and my life over to the care of God as I understood him, it means exactly that. Now I have one source of supply. I have one power, and it isn't me. I have one God in my life. And it's understood that this power is a God because Step Two says this power can do what I can't do and Step Three calls this power "God." Now I have something going for me. Step Three is where I learned to pray. I was at a stag meeting in San Fernando, and I was having great difficulty because I had no belief in a power other than me. There was another alkie there, and he talked real well. He talked sanely, all the time. He talked about today's life all the time. He praised his family, his wife, his kids, and everybody else. Instead of tearing things apart, he was talking good. I watched him week after week. He never changed. I would walk in red-faced, angry, because I just got done fighting with some son of a gun around the corner. But he never changed.

He always talked good. So one day I asked him, "How come you're so different from me? Why are you the way you are?" And he said, "I used to be like you, but now I have a power in my life, which is God. And this power is doing for me what I couldn't do myself. Why don't you try him? Whatever you got doesn't seem to be working." So he was telling me to believe. And he was telling me to pray. I asked him, "How do you pray? What do you call him? When do you do it? Where do you do it? What should I believe in?" He said, "Believe that he'll come into your life, and he'll do for you what he's done for me."

So I went home, and I got down by the bed and kneeled. I started talking to God. I started praying. I felt funny, my blood boiled, and I didn't want to do it. I didn't like it. I shut the door and didn't want anybody to find out I'm doing it. I couldn't do it at home. But I went to work and started talking to this power that fellow called God. I called on God and I asked him, "Would you please help me with my anger and hostility? I'm mad again. I'm hateful again. I'm getting upset. Please help me with my anger. Please help me with this. Please help me with that." I kept talking to God this way. That's all I did. That's the only prayer I offered. I didn't do it at home. I didn't do it in my car. But I could do it at work. The next thing, the guys at work said, "Bob, let's go get some coffee with donuts at the drive-in next door." Now these guys wouldn't have nothing to do with me before. They wouldn't even look at me. I was like a rattlesnake. You wanted to make sure I was in a good mood before you said hello to me. So the next thing, we're telling jokes. Every now and then, I started talking to God again. "I'm sorry, God, I left you. I haven't been back for an hour. Please forgive me. I'm back. Would you still be with me? Would you still help me?" Well, I was doing something then, only I didn't know it. I was doing an application of a principle, and I didn't even know it. Nobody would tell me about this application. They wouldn't show me how to do it. They wouldn't explain it, lay it out, say here it is.

I had to find my way by trial and error. I would have it, and then I would lose it. Have it, lose it. Have it, lose it. But I didn't know why because I hadn't built a character by principles. I built a character by need. I needed help because I was upset and angry, so I asked God to help me with that. But my character never changed. I didn't know I could change, if only I would do something by application. If I turned the application of this step into a way of life, if I could learn to pray without being mad, if I wanted to have God with me all day long, I would be building a new character. But I didn't know about this application. I thought I had to call on God because I was in trouble. So I would talk to God when I was in trouble. Even so I was having such success with my anger and hostility, I started to wonder if I couldn't have more. What if I went for broke? And that's when I realized I can pray wherever I am. Like right now. God is here right now, for each and every one of us. Because I talk to him. Because I ask him to be here. I acknowledge his presence.

This relationship is for all of us. It isn't just for me. I don't pray because I'm in trouble, because there is something special going on and God is needed. That's not it. This relationship is a way of life. No matter where I am—whether I'm going into surgery, whether I'm looking at my wife laying in a casket, or whether I'm just plain happy—I can pray. Otherwise prayer becomes something you do for a reason. It's not a way of life.

The God-consciousness that I must have in my life starts in Step Three. God-consciousness is about practicing God's presence, not my presence. It's talking to something other than myself. This character building comes from applying these Steps. It doesn't come from attending a lot of meetings or from reading a lot. This character building is a total application for a way of life, in the day I'm in, always in the day I'm in. I can't draw from yesterday's happiness or yesterday's success. Whether it's the middle of the day, the beginning of the day, or the end of the day, my disease needs to be treated now. Because that's when I need help.

These Steps grow. They grow deep, deep, deep. Life out there keeps changing. Situations change. There are many variables all the time. So I have to build a character that can do the right thing for one event today, and the next day, and for the rest of my life. As long as my heart's beating, this program of recovery is guaranteed by God.

Here are some frequently asked questions about this Step.

▲ You said that Step Three named the power greater than self as "God." Why is this naming significant?

For me, I had such a quarrel with needing something ther than myself. I froze. For the first two-and-a-half years of belonging to this program, I couldn't say the Lord's Prayer because it referred to a God. They'd say, "Bob, would you lead us in the Lord's Prayer," and I would just stand there. I'd still be standing there if somebody else didn't pick up on it. I couldn't pray to a God, and I didn't think he was something I needed to have in my life. I was so darn programmed to fight, to argue, to be defiant, to be angry, to be hostile, I couldn't do it. I never wanted to give in to God. I didn't want to say, "I need God," or anything like that. I had a big, big problem, and it was always about the same thing. G-O-D. I thought that if I needed God, it meant that I couldn't stand on my own feet. And that would make me less of a man.

So I had a terrible, terrible mind. But in the Twelve by Twelve on page 109 it says, "So, practicing these steps, we had a spiritual awakening about which finally there was no question. Looking at those who were only beginning and still doubted themselves, the rest of us were able to see the change setting in. From great numbers of such experiences, we could predict that the doubter who still claimed that he hadn't got the spiritual angle, and who still considered his well loved AA group the higher power, would presently love God and call him by name." Now all of these words are proven. They are already there. That means that others before me had the same darn problem I had. They had the same darn thought process. They had the mind that would take them right back to the sewer, and yet the Big Book on page 17 says that "we have discovered a common solution. We have a way out on which we can absolutely agree, and upon which we can join in brotherly and harmonious action."

What is the common solution? The common solution is calling God by name. Praying to God. Identifying God. When the Big Book talks on page 93 about having your own conception of God, provided that it makes sense to you, it says that your God must be a power greater than yourself and that you must live by spiritual principles. Your God can be whatever you want. You don't have to call him by name right away. Later on, though, you will.

▲ Is your will the way you think when you're doing what God wants? Or is your will the way you think when you're doing what self wants? How do you tell the difference?

There is no such thing as two separate wills. Now I used to wonder how to tell the difference between my will and God's will. When the disease is not being treated, there is such a thing as your will. That's what brought you here. That's where your life is in the disease. That's where you're damaged. That's where the harm is. That's were you're upset again. When you're in recovery, your will is in alignment with God's will. Then you find that you are happy. That's what the Steps are about. Your life is smooth. Everything is going well. That's what the spiritual principles are about and that's what application is about. My will can't be in the picture as something separate from God's will. No way. I would have to be the power again. I would have to redo and relive and remake the world the way it was before, and I don't want to do that. All through the literature, it talks about God's will. Look at your own track record. When you're upset, who's making you upset? You are, because you are up to your old tricks. When you're happy, what changed? You did. You put your will in alignment with God's will.

▲ How do you get willingness, in the day you're in?

Willingness is a character principle that I must live by. We're not talking about being willing to continue to live in misery and pain. We're talking about being willing to do more, even when you think you're failing. Even when you think there is nothing going on. We're talking about the willingness to trust in God. That's how your faith is built. We're talking about the willingness to act. We're not talking about the willingness to do nothing. We're not talking about being willing to have God feed you while you do nothing, while you sit in a closet waiting to see how many hot dogs God will stuff through the keyhole. It won't happen. You must develop the quality of willingness in character. You don't give up or quit. Nothing will happen. You must be willing to go to any length, right now. Today. In whatever is happening. "Willingness" is a good word for me. It's a word in my language. It's one we're going to continue to talk about.

▲ Please explain what you mean by "God as I understood him" versus "God as I understand him."

Step Three and Step Eleven both refer to "God as we understood him," and they're both emphasized in the same way. Now Step Two is saying that I have to have an open mind. I'm going to have to quit debating and arguing with life. I'm going to have to believe in something other than me, and then I can have soundness of mind. So Step Three says, "I'm going to make a decision to turn my will and my life over to the care of God as I understood him," not to "God as I understand him." Understood. It's understood from Step Two that there are two powers, me and a power greater than me. It's understood that the power of self is going to hurt you and the power greater than self is going to help you. This principle must be understood. You better be over here with a power greater than yourself. You don't try to understand God in the sense of trying to understand the who, what, where, how, and why the power is or anything like that. This step requires a trust and a belief that I couldn't get past in the beginning—until I started to have things happen to me that never happened before. They didn't just happen really. The moment I called upon God, I was helped immediately. It's not a question of understanding what's going on. It's understood that I better turn my will and my life over to this God. It's understood that every time I do so, I get good results. Understood is not understand. This distinction is important. I'm not trying to understand the power of God, where it's at, or how it is. I'm not trying to analyze or look at things or tear them apart. All I know is that if I offer God a prayer, if I ask for help, I'm helped. And I'd be a fool not to ask for help. It's understood that God can do what I can't do.

▲ Is talking to God sincerely and asking God for help enough to keep your God-consciousness?

No. I used to think so. I used to get down on my knees, pray to God, get up from my knees, and leave God when I left the bedroom. I'd go to work and act like a fool. So no, it isn't enough to just talk to God. Step Three doesn't ask you if you want to do Step Three. Instead, Step Three talks about making a decision. Turn your will and your life over to the care of God as we understood him. This decision isn't a pick-and-choose thing. You must stay with God. It isn't a thing that runs hot and cold. It isn't one minute you want to do it, and the next you don't want to do it. There's no such thing as that. As an alcoholic with alcoholism, you better have self-discipline. You better pay attention. It means your life will be saved.

Part 3

Cleansing the Mind

On Step Four

The Courage To Look Inwardly

Made a searching and fearless moral inventory of myself.*

For a long time, I didn't know the purpose of Step Four. It says that you have to make "a searching and fearless" *moral* inventory. Now I had to look up this word, "moral," in the dictionary. "Moral" has to do with whether something is right or wrong, good or bad. I had to make a searching and fearless moral inventory of what was inside me, inside my mind. That is where I live, in my mind. I have to find out whatever I have or use in my mind today.

Now I started my inventory by looking at my relationships with people who were close to me. My mother, my father, my brothers, my sisters, my wife, my co-workers, and my employees. But this searching and fearless moral inventory had to be about me, not about them. Maybe they locked me in a closet or kicked me in the behind. But that didn't matter. For me, what mattered was what I was using to live in the day I was in. I had to learn that my defects of character were things that I do I should not do, not things that were done to me. I can't blame my behavior on things that were done to me in the past.

*For the sake of my own recovery, I changed the Steps to first-person singular.

Step Four is about a moral inventory taken in the day I'm in. I have to look at what's in my mind, whether it got there when I was a kid or whether it got there yesterday. It makes no difference. If it's in my mind today, I have to look at it.

For me, Step Four is about learning why I'm like I am in the day I'm in. Why am I angry today? Why is my life unmanageable today? What are my defects of character?

Personally, I don't think Step Four is a hard Step to do. Nor do I think it is a hard Step for the other alcoholics I work with. That's because you don't have to search very hard for these defects of character. These are things that are in your mind. You know about them; it's not hard for you to identify them. You can identify these things by the way you act, by your behavior, by the way you treat people.

Now at one time, I was one of the most jealous people on earth. And one of the angriest. Now these weren't conditions I found myself in now and then. I was jealous and angry all the time. It didn't make any difference when my jealousy and anger started. It could have started in a barroom. Or it could have started when I was five years old. Who knows? The important thing for me was to recognize that on this day I was a jealous and angry person.

Why take an inventory? Why make a "searching and fearless moral inventory"? What is the purpose? There must be a purpose. I never knew who I was. I never knew what was wrong with me. I never knew that I have defects of character that I display wherever I go. I display the character I am. So I had to start writing about that character. I don't think this Step is that difficult with a little self-honesty and self-discipline and provided you don't want to live the way you've been living.

Some alcoholics make a big deal out of this Step. They put their inventory in the trunk of their car and lock it up for six months. They don't want to face who they are. But the inventory is already there. It's my character. I don't have to add anything to it. It's the way I look at things. It's the way I judge, think, act. And it doesn't make any difference whether your list of defects of character is short or a mile long. If you use one defect of character, you do damage. You damage your self first and then others around you.

You warp your mind. Referring to Step One, the Twelve by Twelve says, "Glass in hand, we warped our minds" (21). Referring to Step Two, page 33 says, "Some will be willing to term themselves 'problem drinkers,' but cannot endure the suggestion they are mentally ill." (33). And referring to Step Four, pages 42 and 43 say:

> Step Four is our vigorous and painstaking effort to discover what these liabilities in each of us have been, and are. We want to find out exactly how, when, and where our natural desires have warped us. We wish to look squarely at the unhappiness this has caused others and ourselves.

To find my defects of character, I had to make a list. I put my mother first, then my father, my brothers, my sisters, and so on down the line. I put them on my list first because these were the people who were closest to me. I could see my behavior toward them more easily than I could see it toward others. I'm not talking about their behavior. My behavior. After I get done looking at my behavior toward my family members, I can go on to others. Bosses. Guys I work with. And so on.

Now when I make this list, I'm trying to find out what makes me tick. I'm trying to find out what's inside me. I'm trying to identify my defects of character. I'm trying to identify a character that's defective. Instead of doing something one way, a way that works, my character will do it another way. When I should be kind, I can't be kind. I don't have the kindness in me to be kind. It's a quality that I don't carry. And that's because I live by my defects.

When I got into this program, I brought my character with me, with all of its defects. Unfortunately, I couldn't identify those defects right away. Step Four gives me the chance to do that. That's possible because I've done Step Three. When I made a decision to turn my will and my life over to the care of God as I understood him, I could do something I couldn't do before. I found a power in me, called God, and I could ask this God to be with me, to take care of me, my will and my life. Then I could take this moral inventory.

A long time ago, I could get away with a lot of things because I didn't know any better. I was sober, but I could lie to you and I wouldn't even feel bad about it. As time went on, I learned how to do other things and I didn't feel bad about them either. When I started to apply these Steps, I got in touch with a power I called God. I asked him to help me write about me. I learned to write down that I was impatient, that I was angry, that I was lying to people. Soon I knew better and couldn't get away with these things anymore. I started to have a different life.

When you apply these Steps, you are building a new character by principles. These Steps go in order—one, two, three, four, five, and six-because they show you how to build character step by step. They show you how to build a new character with principles. Not with principles that are in a book but with principles that are in your life by application. These principles become a total way of thinking, a way of acting, a way of being.

That is why I can handle some things today that I could never have handled yesterday. I can go through difficult days and still have success. Some of the things that happen to me I don't like. Some of the things that happen are scary. But I can still go through them and not lose my mind. That's because I'm not going through them with my fears or with my old memories. I'm going through these experiences with the help of a higher power. Step Three was the foundation. You have to turn your will and life over to the care of God as you understood him. You have to take Step Three to change your character. You can't change your character by yourself. You can't change your character by the force of your will. You can't. It's impossible.

Step Four can be a long Step because you're going into your history. It goes into your yesterdays and into explanations of what your character defects are. It doesn't have to be long provided you know how to identify and list your defects of character. The best definition I've heard of a defect of character is that it is something you do that you should not do. For example, I am an angry person. I show anger. I live the anger. It is something I know how to use. So anger is a defect of character for me. Being angry all the time is something I shouldn't do.

To make your searching and fearless moral inventory, just put down defects of character like I did. I wrote them down first in connection to my loved ones. And then I find out that some defects of character are used with strangers, not just with my mother and father and so on. In this way, I learn a great deal about me and about the way I think in the day I'm in. Maybe I'm out on the freeway. Or maybe I'm in a market. All of a sudden I get angry. I get hostile. I get impatient. I get real critical. Maybe the line's too long. Maybe they're in the "nine items or less line" and have ten items in their basket. Something happens to me. I realize I don't know how to not get angry because anger is the only way I know. So it is becoming clear to me that anger is a defect of character.

Step Four is a Step that I can walk and talk in the day I'm in. I don't have to be angry. I don't have to show my defects of character. If and when my defects come up, and they will, they don't have to stay. I have a method I can apply. I don't have to feed on my defects. I don't have to energize them. I don't have to live with them. Today, I can't harbor anything against anybody. I can't give those feelings life. I won't entertain those thoughts.

You have to have self-honesty for this Step. You have to learn to see these defects of character. If you don't see them, if you don't identify them and write them down, you are doomed to keep repeating them. But with Step Four, even if you do goof up, you recognize that the mistake is something you did not do intentionally. Maybe you hurt someone, but you recognize that you didn't hurt them deliberately and you have a genuine interest in correcting the harm done. You have something going for you now. As you go a little bit farther, you are going to realize that you can have a fulfilling relationship with another human being. This could be your son or daughter, your wife or husband, your mother or father, or a total stranger. It doesn't matter. As a way of life, this program will affect all your relationships. This method is a guarantee for each one of us. You don't have to live in struggle and pain and yesterday's mistakes.

Let's answer some frequently asked questions about Step 4.

▲ Are you saying that it's not important to go back to the past but it is important to see the defects of character in us today?

No, I'm not saying that. I'm saying that you should write down everything in your life today, whether it came from yesterday, yesteryears, yesterchildhood. To write it down, you don't need to work at creating memories. You don't have to try to remember that your mother whipped you when you were little or locked you in a closet at some point. You can go on searching for those things forever and never find your defects of character. Whether something started for you in high school, grade school, or in your early childhood doesn't matter. If it's in your mind today, write it down. It isn't necessary for you to know how it got there or when it got there. What's necessary is for you to apply the Steps, every one of them, and to do what each Step tells you to do.

▲ How do you work Step Four in the day you're in?

The application of Step Four—and you can say this about the application of any Step—has to be a way of life. It has to be a method of living by a power, which is God. This way of life isn't a pie-in-the-sky thing that you might get to someday. This was of life is a now thing, right now. We have to come to this program and find a way of life that will treat alcoholism. When I treat my alcoholism, I treat my whole life. But the primary purpose, and this has to stay primary, is to treat my disease of alcoholism. If you treat your alcoholism first, the problems that follow from your alcoholism will no longer be there. They aren't necessary anymore.

You have to live by principle. You have to go in order, in a logical order, from Step One to Step Two to Step Three to Step Four, all the way to Step Twelve. I have to make a searching and fearless moral inventory of my whole being and my mind. I have to write about what happened in my life, not what I thought happened or what might have happened, but what happened because of the way I think and act.

One way I can take this inventory is to start looking at relationships. That is the beginning. I always get my babies to start with their mother, their father, their brothers, their sisters, anybody close, so they can identify things without too much searching. What was it like when you treated your family rotten, while you were drunk and misbehaving? Let's put that down on paper. Let's write down exactly what you were like, as an alcoholic with alcoholism. What made you act the way you acted and think the way you thought? Why did you mistrust somebody? Why did you get angry at them? Why did you get jealous of them? In an inventory, you write down the things you do, even if they came from yesterday. Why do I hold the thoughts about you that I hold? Maybe you have tattoos, and I don't like you. Why should I have a thought like that? Now, I am taking an inventory of me, of what is disturbing me, of what bothers me, in the day I'm in.

▲ You say, "Start with your mother and your father and list all your resentments." How do you go from that column to listing your defects of character? I'm missing something. I tend to get stuck on all the victimization episodes in my life.

To my way of thinking, there are three columns. In the first column, you list the people; in the next column you list the problem; in the last column you list the defect. To my way of thinking, I can't look at myself directly and see an angry person. I just can't do it. I can't look at myself directly and be able to list those defects of character. What I can do is look at the people I've lived with, see how I've behaved with them, and identify my defects of character that way.

What you're saying and what I'm saying are two different things. What you're wanting to do is look at how bad the world treated you and pounded you and hurt you and then you can say you got your defects of character from that treatment. I'm not talking about that. What I'm talking about is how I built myself. I didn't build my character when I was in kindergarten. I built it when I was about fifteen years old. I was starting to live in the world on my own. I did things. I made things happen. I bought a car. I bought a motorcycle. I'd ride with a bunch of people. I'd go to bars. I'd go to parties. I'd go to a job. My mind began to get distorted when I moved out into the world. I can't blame anyone for the way I am. That's not what Step Four is all about.

▲ When I took my Fourth Step, I looked at how I was raped when I was eight years old. Growing up, I was always angry at the males around me. Now, each time I get married, I won't even let my husband touch me. For me, my defects of character come from that episode.

Let's start all over again. I start by building a new character. To do this, I have to live in the day I'm in. If I had to go through the day thinking about something that happened to me a long time ago, I'd have to get drunk or shoot myself. Every solitary one of us has a track record that we could use to excuse our behavior.

But this program is based on a different concept. Recovery is about the Twelve Steps—a program of recovery for every alcoholic with alcoholism, regardless of what happened to them in the past. Certainly, you have to identify your defects. That's what the Step is about. But if the Step were about uncovering memories that you could dwell on, this wouldn't be a program of recovery. Each one of us would wind up trying to recall all the harms and hurts that have happened to us. How could we live today with our minds so occupied by the ratty things that happened yesterday? We'd never make it.

I know this is a hard message to hear. I know I repeat myself, but this message has got to be heard. Think about it. Does it make sense that there is something so awful in your life that you can never get rid of it? What kind of God would condemn you to live with this terrible thing for the rest of your life? Maybe there is something that you can't get rid of on your own. But I believe in a higher power that can do for me what I can't do for myself. That's why these Steps are in the order they are in. Certainly there are tragedies. All of us have a list of troubles. I have mine, but I can't live in those tragedies and troubles. This is today's life. This is the life in which God says, under his grace, I can be happy, joyous, and free. I don't have to be bitter about something that happened to me in the past, whether it was yesterday or many years ago.

The only way recovery is possible is if you learn to be dependent upon God. Totally dependent. In your every thought, in your every deed, you have to be dependent on God. All day long and in all your affairs. At Step Four, we're not there yet. We're still trying to learn to get there. We're still trying to find those principles that will turn this program of recovery into a way of life.

This program was put here on earth through Dr. Bob and Bill Wilson on June 10, 1935. Since they printed the Big Book in April of 1939, the program of recovery has not changed. The program of recovery is still in the Twelve Steps. You have to look at this now. This is your life. What do you want? Do you want what we have? Are you willing to go to any lengths to get it? I can't do it for you. You can't do it for me. Together we can do it. As it says on page 17 of the Big Book:

> We have a way out, upon which we absolutely can agree, and upon which we can join in brotherly and harmonious action. This is the news that this book carries to those who suffer from alcoholism.

Step Four is there so that you can write down exactly what is in your mind today. If it came from when you were young, if it came from your yesterdays, it's today. Write it down. You're doing the inventory, and then you can see what happens after that.

▲ Can you say something about what it means to be "fearless"?

Making a "searching and fearless moral inventory" means that you're not afraid to be open. You have to stay open, wide open. I don't mean that you broadcast your defects to everyone. But I am talking about being open, especially to a sponsor. You have to open up. You can't keep things hidden. If you make a searching and fearless moral inventory, you're not afraid of what's in there. You're not afraid to tell it to somebody. Opening up is going to set you free. Opening up is what will make your tomorrows free of fear. You won't have memories that drive you nuts. They just won't be there.

▲ Can you explain the fear list?

Every defect of character has a fear associated with it. If you fear something, you haven't accepted it. If you look at any fear you have, now, you'll find something that you're not accepting. You have to write this down. Every defect has a fear associated with it. The fear does not produce the defect. It's a consequence of the defect.

I remember one man from Denver, Colorado. He had eighteen months in the program. He did an inventory, but he didn't make out a fear list. He was running so scared. He couldn't stand to work. He was even afraid to talk to his wife. He was frightened all the time, and he didn't know why. He had no basis for being as frightened as he was. He recognized his defects. He wrote about them. He offered them to God. But he never looked at what happened because of the defect. He was afraid of being found out.

Look in the third column of the moral inventory approach found on page 65 of the Big Book. It's about fears. You have to identify these fears. They are just as important as the defects.

▲ How do you know what your defects of character are? On page 65 of the Big Book, the first column lists somebody you relate to: your Mom, for example. The second column lists what's going on: maybe she hit you when you were five. The third column gets to the fears. How do you find the defect of character?

It isn't that your Mom hit you when you were five. It's that your relationship with your mother generates some fears in you now. Maybe it affects your sexual relationships today. You have to be looking at how things are affecting you this day, today. You can't be doing an inventory of your mother. You start with your mother because you can look at your relationship with her and find out what's wrong with you. You don't judge your mother. That isn't going to help you.

Try not to be scared of doing an inventory. You can do them more than once. The Big Book mentions annual or semi-annual inventories. I know guys who do them maybe two or three times a year. Generally, these inventories are no more than recognizing that something needs to be talked about. I know a guy in Sacramento who did an inventory because he walked into his house and saw a sink full of dirty dishes. He's got a beautiful home, a beautiful wife, a beautiful daughter, and all he can think about when he gets home from work is a sink full of dirty dishes. So he decides maybe there is something he needs to look at.

Check this out for yourself. See if this inventory business will work for you. These Steps were put in the order they are in for a reason. If they weren't there, every one of us would have to live in pain. My wife died when I was three-and-a-half years sober. I never once apologized to her. When I was ready, I couldn't wake her up to do it. But these Steps have enabled me to go on and live my life and see that this is a good world. This program will guarantee every one of you a way of life. Go for it. If you don't go for it today, it won't happen.

▲ Explain the difference between the "moral inventory" mentioned in Step Four and the "personal inventory" mentioned in Step Ten.

In Step Ten, you do a personal inventory of the day you live in, as you live in the day. In Step Four, you're doing an inventory of the character you brought here. In Step Ten, you do an inventory so that you don't start to build another character out of your old defects, in the day you're in. It's something I do, in the moment I'm in, in the day I'm in, at any time I'm in. Step Four is an inventory of the character already established. My defects are there. I'm not looking at some defects and hoping I don't do them. I do them. That's the way I operate. That's the way I live. So that's why I have to go on to the Fifth Step.

On Step Five

Being One With God And Man

Admitted to God, to myself, and to another human being the exact nature of my wrongs.*

Step Five, I believe, is harder to do than Step Four. In Step Four, all I have to do is identify who the heck I really am, in the day I'm in. Why am I what I am? Am I jealous? Am I angry? Do I blow my lid all the time? That's what it's all about, making a fearless and searching moral inventory. It's a right-from-wrong thing. It's "I should do this and not that." When I identify what I should not do, I've identified a defect of character. Now you might have a long list or you might have a short list. It doesn't make any difference. The character that uses these defects does the damage. In this life that I live in, I hurt people. I do the same thing over and over again because I can't do anything different. I'm always the same character.

Now I have to learn what the principles of this program mean so that I can do the opposite of my defects of character. Instead of telling lies, I have to learn to tell the truth. Instead of being somebody that's jealous, I have to learn why I'm jealous. And I was a jealous character. I almost killed a man

*For the sake of my own recovery, I changed the Steps to first-person singular.

one time, in his own bed with his wife and his two kids in the house, because I thought he was screwing around with my wife. Whether he was or not, I have no idea to this day. But I thought he was.

With my defects of character and my thought processes, I hurt and harm everything around me. I'm loaded with things that are wrong with me. Everything about my thinking and behavior is to the extreme. I never do anything just a little bit. I do everything the whole way. This jealousy is a defect of character. Did you ever start something and not be able to quit, even though you're causing a lot of damage? You have to finish it. You go so far you wish you hadn't been born. This is about your character. Your character can't do any different because it's built on defects. To learn about these defects, you must write about them. You must put them down on paper. That's the Fourth Step.

Now with the Fifth Step, you have to admit to God, to yourself, and to another human being the exact nature of your wrongs. This is hard because you have to admit something to yourself. You have to understand what it means to "admit" something to yourself and others here. I learned, even when I was drinking, that I could "admit" to things and get off the hook for a while. That's not what we're talking about here. We're talking about how you admit something to yourself and accept the truth of it inside yourself. This is hard. Accepting the truth gets into building the new character. You're not a self-deceiving, self-lying character. This is a character full of self-honesty. Now, you start to realize that your performance is changing in the day you're in.

Accepting who I am was hard for me. It was something I didn't want to do. I could admit most things to just about anyone, but there were a couple of things I swore I'd never admit to anyone. But there came a time when I had to. I had to do it because my recovery couldn't go any farther without doing it. That's the thing. You have to be totally honest and reveal yourself for who you really are. You're going to have to do this with another human being. You're going to have to work while knowing who you are and accepting who you are.

Self-honesty was a difficult thing for me. Right when I was new in the program back in Cleveland, Ohio, my sponsor hit me real hard with self-honesty. I had to learn what self-honesty is. He made sure. He said, "Don't you ever tell me a lie." He had his finger in my nose. "Don't you ever tell me a lie. Let's get off on the right foot here, right now." He said, "I'm the expert, not you. Don't you think for one minute that you can lie to me." That was a principle he drove home. If we were going to have a relationship based on recovery, I had to tell the truth, regardless. Now this started me off in a different kind of world. I wouldn't dream of telling him a lie. I was scared to tell him a lie. I didn't even know what he would do. This is important. If your life is anything like mine, it's governed by a lot of phony crap. I was used to treating somebody a certain way because they were a certain person. No way. You can't do that as an alcoholic with alcoholism. You can't. Maybe somebody else can do it, but I can't do it. It hurts me. It stops me. It kills me. It makes my world a ratty world, a place where I don't want to be. I don't know why. I want to blame everybody but me. But it's me, the character that I am. I can't trust me because of my defects. I said before, I'm like a rattlesnake. One minute I'm feeling good. I'm fine. But the next minute I'm feeling bad and you better stay away from me. Why? What kind of character am I? Why should I be governed like that? Why should I be happy and then, all of a sudden, be sad? Why can I accept you and then, all of a sudden, I can't accept you? My defects of character are coming to the surface.

When you admit to God, to yourself, and to another human being the exact nature of your wrongs, you get to the place where you start accepting yourself as you really are. That's what happened to me. I know who I am. I know what I'm up to today. I know where I'm going, and I know how to get there.

▲ Can you take Step Five with a member of the clergy or a psychiatrist or should you do it with your sponsor?

I'd rather do the Step with my sponsor. I'd rather do the Step with somebody who knows alcoholism and who knows what I'm about—and my sponsor is going to know more than somebody outside of the program. But do whatever will allow you to do the most with the Step. Do whatever will make you feel better.

▲ How do you take Step Five in the day you're in?

When you admit to God, to yourself, and to another human being the exact nature of your wrongs, you're building the new character for today. You do this so that you can live your life in the present rather than in the past. You do this so that what happened yesterday no longer affects you today. Maybe somebody treated you badly yesterday, but you're still thinking about it today. When you meet them today, you react to them based on your memory. And it makes you miserable. How would you like to live without that memory making you retaliate? How would you like to live for today? You would have no bad memories. You wouldn't have to waste today blaming people, accusing them, and holding grudges against them. This program is all about freeing a mind that's governed by yesterday's life, yesterday's performance, and yesterday's people. These bad memories stop me from being who I could be today. Step Five is about freeing yourself from these memories and learning to live free. This is character building.

Keep in mind that you don't build the new character completely in Step Five. You do it in Steps One through Twelve. But you can live your life in the day you're in by doing Step Five. You don't have to wait until you're finished with all Twelve Steps to be okay. This is important. The program of recovery is like a closed circuit. Once you've begun the application in Step One, your alcoholism begins to be treated. But you must go forward in Step application.

▲ Should you call somebody in the program on a daily basis to tell them what you said or did on that day? And would that be part of Step Five?

I wouldn't say there is anything wrong with doing that, but I wouldn't say this practice is part of Step Five. No. The Steps are in a certain order and I think there is a reason for that. What is important about Step Five is to be totally dependent on a power greater than myself. Now I can call you everyday, but I have to live with a power greater than you. If I'm too dependent on you, if I think the call itself is going to fix my problems, then I haven't grasped the principle of this Step. I have to have fellowship, but I have to be totally dependent on something besides human power.

On Step Six

A Perfect Release

Was entirely ready to have God remove all these defects of character.*

Having built this new character from Steps One to Five, now I have to realize the purpose of Step Six. I'm entirely ready now to do something about something, and that something has already been established. It's to "have God remove all these defects of character." All of them, not some of them.

I used to have a fit when I read the last two pages of Step Six in the Twelve by Twelve. I thought those pages were giving me a cop-out, a way of letting me take my good old time. I read it for what I thought was there, but what I thought was there really wasn't there. Finally I learned what it meant to have God remove *all* these defects of character. And that the removal of all these defects is necessary and possible. Step Six wouldn't have been put there if it were impossible.

So Step Six comes in the sixth place for a reason. Steps One through Six are all about the disease of alcoholism and everything you need to build this new character. To be

*For the sake of my own recovery, I changed the Steps to first-person singular.

entirely ready to have God remove all your defects of character is something you can do. At one time, I couldn't see the principles and the truth of what we were doing. I just couldn't. I would go to meetings, read the literature, talk with my sponsor, and never look at this concept of character change found in the Steps.

"Were entirely ready to have God remove all these defects of character." This is the program's way of describing the attitude you need to approach this character change. What's an attitude? An attitude is something that's already there. It's fixed. It's permanent. Step Six describes the best possible attitude for beginning this lifetime job. Yes, a lifetime job. The Twelve by Twelve, on page 50, points out that "Step Four is the beginning of a lifetime practice." So in Step Six we become "entirely ready to have God remove these defects of character" forever. On this day, today, no matter how many years I've got in the program, I am entirely ready to have God remove my defects of character. Now this is a guarantee that turns these Steps into a way of life. No matter what happens, even when I make a mistake, I still have the power to become the character that I should be.

Step Six helps me realize this today. I might show you some anger. That's an old defect of character for me and something I know a great deal about. Anger is liable to boomerang back on me at any time of the day, at any time in my life, no matter how many years I've been in this program. But when the anger comes, or any other defect, there is a principle in me that allows me to go ahead and have that corrected. That's because I'm entirely ready to have God remove all these defects of character today, even after all these years in the program. Now these are important things I'm saying. You can find them in the literature. This is a method of living, by a power greater than me, which is God. I can live my life on principles and not flip-flop around. I don't have to give up or wind up thinking, "What the heck is the use? I'll never make it."

Now there are a couple of things in the Twelve by Twelve that are real important to me. On the top of page 64, it talks about how I came to the program in Step One and I wanted God to take care of my drinking. That's all I really wanted. That's all I really knew. Then on page 36, in reference to Step Three, it talks about how dependent I am and how unconscious I am of that dependence. I don't even know what the term "dependency" means, but I still want God to take care of my alcohol. And then on page 37, it says, "But the moment our mental or emotional independence is in question, how differently we behave. How persistently we claim the right to decide all by ourselves just what we shall think and just how we shall act." I want God to be over here handling my alcohol, but I leave everything else alone because I figure I can handle the rest of my life.

And then you get to Step Six where it says to become entirely ready to have God remove all my defects of character. On page 64, speaking of Step Six, the Twelve by Twelve says, "Having been granted a perfect release from alcoholism, why then shouldn't we be able to achieve by the same means a perfect release from any other difficulty or defect? That's the riddle of our existence. Perhaps the full answer lies only in the mind of God." I want God to help me stay sober, but I don't want God to show me the way of life that I have to follow. I don't want him to interfere with any of my pleasures or my wants or anything else like that. The Twelve by Twelve continues:

> But most of our difficulties don't fall under such a [self-destructive] category. Every normal person wants, for example, to eat, to reproduce, to be somebody in the society of his fellows. And he wishes to be reasonably safe and secure as he tries to attain these things. Indeed, God made him that way. He did not design man to destroy himself by alcohol, but he did give him instincts to stay alive."

It also says on page 64:

> In a very complete and literal way, all A.A.'s have 'become entirely ready' to have God remove the mania for alcohol from their lives. And God proceeded to do exactly that.

And then it says that if God has given us a "perfect release" from alcohol, why shouldn't he release us from every other defect? Well, he can, but I don't want him to. I don't want him to because I want my will to be there, and I want my pleasures to be there. Remember, the literature says that "these other difficulties don't fall under such a category." My difficulties weren't about drinking. They were about living. I don't want God messing with my stuff. I just want him to take care of my drinking. That's all.

The literature says, "Every normal person wants, for example, to eat, reproduce, and be somebody in society." Why are they talking about eating? How about asking God to help me so that I don't get as big as a house. Why are they talking about reproducing? Maybe I've got problems with sex. Why are they talking about being somebody? Maybe I want to be a big shot, to get ahead of you, to get some recognition. On page 65 of the Twelve by Twelve, it says:

> Since most of us are born with an abundance of natural desires, it isn't strange that we often let these far exceed their intended purpose. When they drive us blindly, or we willfully demand that they supply us with more satisfactions or pleasures than are possible or due us, that is the point at which we depart from the degree of perfection that God wishes for us on earth. That is the measure of our character defects or, if you wish, our sins.

Someone asked me how to define "defects of character." For me, the way to handle this question is to look at where I do more than what's necessary. Where do I go to extremes, whether I'm drunk or I'm sober? Why do I have to have the assurance of having more of everything. I go out to the store and buy toilet paper. I don't buy one roll; I buy ten. Why can't I buy one and be satisfied with that? How come I store up soap? I store up everything. When I smoked years ago, I used to buy two or three cartons of cigarettes and stick them in the drawer. I was afraid of running out, so I had to make sure I had some backups. My whole life was like that when I was drunk. Then I found out it was like that when I was sober because I was not entirely ready to have God in my life for everything.

It's different today. I'm entirely ready to have God in my life for what I know are my troubles and for what I think are my adversities. How can I be ready to have God remove all of my defects of character forever? Step Six is the "beginning of a lifetime job," as it says in the literature. What is the beginning of a lifetime job? Trying to live in the day I'm in without the rat race. Trying to live, in the day I'm in, so that the things that bothered me before, my defects of character, are not there. They just are not there anymore. But how are they not there? This is important. If I'm entirely ready to have God remove these defects of character, what does that mean? How could I keep using these defects of character if God removed them? And why would he remove them from me if that's what keeps me going, in the day I'm in?

I identified my defects of character in Step Four, accepted them in Step Five, and now I've got to look at Step Six as something that's happening to me right now. This is building character by principles. If I leave out this principle, I'll have to keep facing the same thing over and over again. My defects of character are the only way I know how to act. They are the only way I know how to live. This is a big, big Step because I can't go on to Step Seven unless I do Step Six. So Step Six is a qualifying thing, just like Step Two qualified me to go to Step Three. Without Step Two I couldn't go on to Step Three because I still had the same thing with me all of the time. I was still believing in myself, and Step Three says, no, you have to believe in this here God. Now we're up here in Step Six, and Step Six is strictly the same thing: building character by principles.

On page 66 of the Twelve by Twelve, it says:

> What we must recognize now is that we exult in some of our defects. We really love them. Who, for example, doesn't like to feel just a little superior to the next fellow, or even quite a lot superior? Isn't it true that we like to let greed masquerade as ambition? To think of liking lust seems impossible. But how many men and women speak love with their lips, and believe what they say, so that they can hide lust in a dark corner of their minds? And even while staying within conventional bounds, many people have to admit that their imaginary sex excursions are apt to be all dressed up as dreams of romance.
>
> Self-righteous anger also can be very enjoyable. In a perverse way we can actually take satisfaction from the fact that many people annoy us, for it brings a comfortable feeling of superiority. Gossip barbed with our anger, a polite form of murder by character assassination, has its satisfactions for us, too. Here we are not trying to help those we criticize; we are trying to proclaim our own righteousness.

I talk about how alcoholics mean what they say. Everything an alcoholic says, even me, has a basis. There's something behind it, and I mean what I say. If I jokingly say something to you about your behavior, your nationality, the color of your skin, there's something behind it. I mean it. I don't kid. Alcoholics don't kid. They don't tell jokes. They might come up behind you, slap you on the back and call you a dumb Polack, but they aren't kidding. There's something behind it.

That's the character I have to expose. That's the character I am. I'm not talking about you. I'm talking about how I'm going to fit in this world so that I can live in the world. It's a good world. I have to live in a way that I'm not hurting people. I'm not taking advantage of situations or of you. I have to be responsible, right now, for my actions, my thinking, my life, wherever I am. I have to—otherwise I walk around with a brain that's loaded with anger. It's full of fears. It's full of yesterdays. So I have to do Step Six. I have to be entirely ready to have God do something for me. This is important. This is powerful. Why should I go ahead and think that doing this Step is a reading thing, a memory thing, or something like that? Why can't I have these defects of character, which are keeping me in a world I don't want to be in, removed? I can. I really can. I know I can. I know how to do it. But the removal never is in the future. And it certainly can't come from the past. So what is it? It's an application of doing things today with the principles backing me up in what to do, what to say, and how to say it. In this way I can actually do something today. I can be somebody other than who I am because God makes it possible.

I finally accepted that I can be free from my defects. I can be a new man. I'm way up in Step Six now. Way down in Step Two and Three, I learned about who I am and what I need. Having done Steps Two and Three, I can now go on to Step Six because this old file cabinet in my mind isn't telling me all the things I should say, all the things I should think, and all the things I should do. How would I ask God to do something for me that I can't do for myself? Would I pray to God and then turn around and treat you like dirt? Would I do that? Is that what this step means? Am I allowed to go ahead, in the day I'm in, and do as I darn please because something affects me and I don't like it? I used to think that everything I did was okay because I was sober. I'm sober and working and doing everything right, but I think you're wrong. These are the defects of character that used to make me drink, and now they are the same ones I'm using today. These defects of character don't have anything to do with drinking.

There's so much about character building in Step Six that

has to be exposed. I cannot go any farther past Step Six if there are still defects of character in me that I do not want to let God correct. I'll be stuck where I'm at. I wouldn't dare go any farther because I'd be operating on my own again, just like I was before. I would have to be the power again. I would have to be the same person I've always been. I used to think that over here I have trouble, but over there I'm an angel. Over here everything's fine; over there, there's a problem. can act with vengeance or with a vicious mind over here, but over there I can act happy, joyous, and free. I didn't know this is impossible.

This is impossible because the disease of alcoholism is a complete disease. It's a total disease. It's a mind-controlling disease. It's a method of living. It doesn't come in inches. It doesn't come slow or subtle. Bam! Just like that, it's on you. Just like that. Alcoholism comes on full blast. One thought will trigger it. One thought and self takes over. And self doesn't take over just one place. Self becomes the power again. Here comes all my past. Here comes everything I represent. Me. You only need one thing to trigger it. Before I used to think that I could get away with one area of my life being wrong and have the rest be okay. But I can't. My whole life is wrong. When one part of me is wrong, it's all wrong. This will be more evident in the next Step.

This is important to talk about. I was under the impression that my length of time in sobriety, the number of meetings I attended, the reading I did, and my "working" the Twelve Steps were the things that made my alcoholism get better. But the character can't change that way. It can't change because of the same things that brought me here: a disease of the mind called alcoholism. It's still present. It's an "ism." It was never a "wasm." There is no way you can treat this disease and it's gone. It doesn't go. It's not the kind of thing that goes away. If you and I could lock our disease up in a safe somewhere and walk away from it, free and clear, wouldn't that be something? That would be like getting a head transplant. But it's nothing like that. It just isn't like that at all. This disease is alive. It's an "ism." It's now, and it grows and gets worse. It gets more damaging. This disease gets more powerful because my mind is growing. In sobriety, my mind's better, feels better, knows more, can do more, and can take advantage of people more easily. In sobriety, there's more people around me. So I can hurt you and everyone else, too.

What I'm saying might sound like just words to you. It might sound repetitive. But this disease is repetitive. It's damaging. And it gets worse. So you have to consider this program. It works. I'm a fool if I walk away from experiences or from knowledge of this proven method. I'm a fool because I'm walking right back into my alcoholism. I'm walking right back into my troubles again. I'm right back where I said I'd never go again.

Now I know very well that I don't walk on water. I make mistakes. But today the mistakes I make are not that severe. They're not that damaging because I don't live with them that long. I don't relive them. I don't keep re-doing them. That's what this program is about. It gives me a chance when I make a mistake. If I fall down, I don't have to stay down. I can get up and start again. The power is in the Steps, in the principles, in the character that I am today. I don't have to be where I was. I don't have to be lost and not know what to do or where to go. This program shows you far more than your mind can ever dream. I've been limited all my life and still am, by myself. But this power that's greater than me, this God, this Lord, is not limited. Sometimes I forget and go ahead and think that whatever I do is okay. But all I have to do again is trust in God.

On page 98 of the Big Book, it says:

> Burn the idea into the consciousness of every man that he can get well regardless of anyone. The only condition is that he trust in God and clean house.

I never knew that my house is where I live. It's my mind. page 100 of the Big Book, it refers to "you and the new man." Now what does that mean? "The new man" isn't someone who is brand new to the program. The new man is brand new in the day he's in, with God and the program of recovery. And so it says,

> Both you and the new man must walk day by day in the path of spiritual progress. If you persist, remarkable things will happen. When we look back, we realize that the things which came to us when we got ourselves in God's hands were better than anything we could have planned. Follow the dictates of the higher power and you'll presently live in a new and wonderful world no matter what your present circumstances.

This message is always about the same thing: God doing for us what we couldn't do for ourselves. It's always about a power greater than you and me. Even on page 60 in the Big Book, it says "that God could and would if He were sought." This is the message of the Twelve Steps. This is the message of recovery.

The hardest thing for me to get across is that Step Six is the beginning of a lifetime practice. No matter where I'm at, no matter what's happening to me, no matter what's going down, I still have to have the same thing. I still have to have God in my life helping me, taking things out of my life that are hurting me. This is an attitude. I told you before that you need a fixed attitude. Your attitude needs to be fixed on God, fixed on recovery. I have something now that's proven for me. I don't have to monkey around with it or question the need for God. "Do I need him here or need him there?" This attitude was established a long time ago, in Step Two and then in Step Three. Step Three told me to "turn my will and life over to the care of God as I *understood* Him," and that's something I need to do. It's *understood* that, from this moment on, my life will be based on a power greater than myself, which is God.

I used to be in doomsday all of the time. I was always expecting the worst. I was always looking at life with the attitude that I'm going to lose. I ain't going to make it. I'm broke. I'm in trouble. That's alcoholism thinking. That's the power of self. Right now, I don't think that way. My heavenly father is taking care of me. No harm will come to me right now. No temptation will disturb me or destroy me. That's the grace of God. That's the undeserved gift from God.

Step Six is getting me ready for action, for applying the steps as a way of life and for getting my disease treated. At this point, we've learned a great deal about this program. We've learned about the disease of alcoholism, what's needed, and what we have to do. This is all about the disease that I have in me, as an alcoholic, and here I am in Step Six entirely ready to have God remove all my defects of character. Forever. Forever. That's the purpose of Step Six. It means that I can make a mistake today and God can correct it. I can miss the mark, but I don't have to die because of it. I can miss the mark, but I don't have to kill people because of it. The responsibility that I have in my life today is great. It's really great. And I know it. I can do these things that I'm talking about. It is possible now to be the man I should be, in the day I'm in. I can't be that way by myself. I must have a power greater than myself.

▲ What saved you from the fear of financial insecurity in your life?

I used to run on my own steam, trying to make my life work. I'd try this and that, and I got the idea in my head that I can make this world a world that I want. I push and shove. I try to get whatever I want, money, material possessions. Step Four helped me identify the character that I am, the character that I present to the world.

There is a fear list in Step Four. If I'm always thinking

about obtaining money, property, prestige, and happiness all the time, I'm going to run into trouble. I'm developing a character that is restless, irritable, and discontented. I'm fighting battles that don't need to be fought. If I'm going to have a sound mind, I can't live with these defects of character. Nothing pleases me. I got a mind that can't be satisfied. You have to look at what your mind is like, drunk or sober. My mind can't be satisfied. You can't give me whatever I want to make me right because, whatever you give me, it's wrong. That's why I switch gals all the time. I think, "This gal is a beauty. I'll make it this time. I'll get everything I need if I have her." So I get her and what happens? The world gets cockeyed again, and I have to look for somebody else.

On page 68 of the Twelve by Twelve, it says:

> If we would gain any real advantage on the use of this Step on problems other than alcohol, we shall need to make a brand new venture into open-mindedness. We shall need to raise our eyes toward perfection, and be ready to walk in that direction. It will seldom matter how haltingly we walk. The only question will be, "Are we ready?"

The concept of "open-mindedness" is really important. It is imperative that I keep an open mind. We learned about open-mindedness in Step Two. But now we must make a "brand new venture into open-mindednes," which means that no matter what's going down, no matter how bad things look, even if it looks like doomsday is coming, I must keep an open mind. I bought a GI house over in Canoga Park, California, in March of 1954. The payment was $69 a month, including taxes and insurance. I kept the house twenty years. Now during those twenty years, I used to drive down the street toward my house and I'd think, "I'm going to lose that thing. I ain't going to make it. They're going to take it from me. They're going to repo my house." Can you imagine, I was making $100 a day. Now $100 a day back then was a lot of money. That was my thought process because of the character I was at the time. I was used to living with failure, adversities of different kinds. I was used to struggling and losing. I didn't have the power to do anything else. After I found a higher power, the old thinking process would pop up every now and then. Then, it would take me over, but it wouldn't stay because the principles have become a way of life for me. To keep this message alive, to make this life be what God says it will be, I have to stay with God. I have to stay with God. I have to live with him. I have to go with him. Step Six makes it possible for me to stay with God. If adversity comes now—for me it has meant coming close to death—I don't lose it. There were times when I didn't know what was going on, but I still went back to God. I asked God to stay with me, to help me, to protect me. I still do this today. Right now I have to do this because I have a disease called alcoholism.

There's nothing wrong with my mind now. My mind is fine, but only because God says so. Now that's something to talk about. Maybe you've never spent a day running scared, but let the doctor tell you, "You're going to die. Say goodbye to your family." That's what they did to me, and what happened. I lost it for a little while, maybe a couple of hours. And then it came back. What came back was no more than the strength of God. The assurance from God. The God-consciousness that told me, "No matter what happens, I am going to take care of you." This assurance in turn set me free from me, and this is what I wanted all the time and never knew it. If I can only learn that this God is the only place I'll ever need to go, I'll be all right. I must be totally dependent on God, and this will happen a little later in the Steps.

▲ It's natural for me to practice my defects of character rather than practicing the presence of God. Do these defects of character reside in the unconscious mind?

Yes, positively. They really do. The purpose of this program is to treat alcoholism, and alcoholism is a disease of the mind. As an alcoholic, I've got a mind that's hurt. There's not a darn thing I can do about these defects of character except build a new character. I have to build a new character through a program of recovery, which is God and the Steps. This program is always talking about how you can be a new character and how you can do things that you couldn't do before. With this program of recovery, you build a new character with soundness of mind, sanity of mind, wholeness of mind. This character building started way back in Step Two.

I don't think the way I used to think. My mind goes in the sewer all the time, by itself. I don't want it there, and I don't need to have it there, but I can't keep it out of there by myself. It's impossible. But this program of recovery enables me to do what is needed. There is a guarantee here for each one of us. And the guarantee is always the same: My heavenly Father will take care of me. No harm will come to me. This is what the Steps are for. This is a good world. This is a world that doesn't attack me. It doesn't hurt me. It doesn't harm me.

I can't just say that and make myself believe it. Those are just words. Words don't mean nothing. What's going on inside me is what counts. I know for sure that, right now, the life I have is genuine. It's real. It's going on. It's not something that starts and stops. It's not something that I'm going to lose all of a sudden.

▲ What does the word "character" mean? Is it an action or a person?

Well, like I said before, I didn't use to like the word

"character" because I associated it with trouble and adversity. People used to say, "Don't trust that character. He's no good, because he'll turn on you."I was trouble. "Character" isn't just a word. "Character" is who I am and the way I live. Now think about this word in application. Do you think I could go to bed with that troublesome character and think good thoughts? Do you think I could do that? I never could before. The minute I got wrapped up in my self, I turned on the world. The whole world sucked. It didn't make any difference if I had money or I didn't; if I had a car or I didn't; if I had a girl or I didn't; if I had a home or I didn't. I had a motorhome, motorcycles, dune buggies. I had everything, and I was still the same sober as I was when I was drunk. You could give me all those things or take them away, and it made no difference. I'd still turn on you because my character never changed.

▲ How do I distinguish my character defects from my character assets?

People in the program used to tell me to write down my character assets as well as my defects. I don't buy it. I learned a long time ago that, in the world I live in, it wasn't the good things that were hurting me. It was the bad things. It wasn't my goodness that kept me drunk. It was the badness in me. I didn't have that goodness in me. I couldn't produce anything genuine, anything real. Everything I produced came from an injured mind, a sick mind, a distorted mind, a mind from the sewer, a mind from selfish self. What good can come out of that? What asset could come out of that mind? Nothing. Not in my life. My goodness never got me drunk, but my badness did. My badness kept me in the world of hurts and harms.

▲ To gain an open mind is one thing, but how do you keep your mind open forever?

Well, forever is only today. That's the way the program

explains it. What we have in this program is a daily reprieve, not a lifetime reprieve. I can only live my life in the day I'm in. If I had the power to take this stuff into every area of my life, into forever, I wouldn't need help in the first place. You have to establish your reason for coming here right away. In Step Two, before you are even qualified to go on to Step Three, you have a God in your life. There's no way you can look at this program of recovery like it's a future thing. I don't know what the heck to do tomorrow because tomorrow isn't here yet. But I sure know what to do today. I must have an open mind today. I must use these principles today. Otherwise, today is the day I get drunk. Today is the day I do harm. Not tomorrow.

▲ Does "trust in God and clean house" mean "trust in God and take an inventory"?

Sure, it means exactly that. Now I used to think about this literally—like I had to trust in God and keep my home clean. But now I understand that my house is my mind. I've got a mind that needs to be straightened out. I have a mind that's a power. It's where I live. I live in my mind, not in a building. The whole world is in my mind. That's where I can find disaster, trouble, true happiness, success, women. They're all in my mind.The slogan assures us that if we trust in God and look inside to see what's going on, we are on the right track.

Part 4

A Brand-New World

On Step Seven

The Art of Giving

Humbly asked Him to remove my shortcomings.*

Step Seven can be misleading because of the way it is stated. In the beginning, I didn't know what Step Seven meant because it referred to removing my shortcomings. I thought this meant there was something inside me, like a "defect," that had to be taken out. But that's not the way it is. If you look at the word "shortcomings," you'll see that it refers not to things that I have inside of me but things that I lack. Things that I'm short on. Things that are not there. So when the Step talks about "removing" those things, it's talking only about removing whatever is stopping me from doing something that I should be doing.

Now a long time ago, someone talked to me about Step Seven. At that point, I had already had a lot of time in the program. I had done a lot of service work and Twelve Stepping. I'll never forget the way he approached me. He told me he thought there was something missing in my life. "Why don't you hear me out?" he asked. "Don't quarrel with this. Just see if there is something here you can benefit from."

*For the sake of my own recovery, I changed the Steps to first-person singular.

And then he proceeded to tell me the difference between defects of character and shortcomings. "Defects of character," he said, "were things I did that I shouldn't do, and shortcomings were things I should do that I'm not doing."

Then he gave me a lesson about a toothpick. "If there is a toothpick on the floor of your home, pick it up."

And I asked him, "Why?"

"Because, if you don't, someone else will have to pick it up." He was trying to show me that in this world where I live, there is a performance I must give. This business about picking up a toothpick isn't really about picking up a toothpick. It's about doing something that I should do. This is something that is going to help me in my life, in the character that I am, and it will apply to all the other areas of my life. This performance was hard for me to accept at first, but it got easier as time went on. As I lived life knowing these things, my life became different because of what I was doing. Now this performance I give will be different than what I normally do. I've always been a taker. I've always been looking out for me. I've always taken things, not just material things. Even in my friendships, I've been a taker. I got selfish and self-centered years ago. Here, in Step Seven, having done Steps One through Six, I'm still that same selfish character. I'm still looking out for me first. "You take care of me, and we'll be friends." I always look at life from the wrong side of the stick. I'm perverse. I'm always trying to make something happen so that I get something out of it.

As far as shortcomings went, I started out with simple things. I would recognize something to do, and then I'd do it because I wanted to do it. I'm not going to do things under protest. I have to want to do things. I can get there, but I'm not good at knowing what to do. So I need help in recognizing what to do. Things like holding a door open for somebody. Now I used to hold doors open for people but always because I felt like I was forced to do it. In this program, I learned I was responsible for doing things because of the character that I am with God.

What I am talking about is important. A long time ago—this was way before there were many street people around—I would run into people who would hit me up for money. A guy would bum me for money, and I'd bite his head off. I would just rip him apart, wondering why he didn't go to work and that sort of thing. When I got sober, I had the same attitude. Certain places I'd be okay. Other places I wouldn't be okay. Then my life became important to me. I started living in a new world. God's world. I began giving of myself, not necessarily monetarily, but by contributing to the world.

This was a new venture for me, a new venture into open-mindedness. This contributing is what Step Seven is about. I was in a place where I couldn't count my blessings. I had things I bought with money, but I didn't recognize them as blessings. I wasn't aware of what God had given me in the world I lived in. Today I can make money and have things, but I know where they come from. They don't come from my work just because I'm a smart guy or because I work long hours. These are things God has given me in the world that I live in.

Now regarding Step Seven, the Twelve by Twelve says:

> Since this Step so specifically concerns itself with humility, we should pause here to consider what humility is and what the practice of it can mean to us.
>
> Indeed the attainment of greater humility is the foundation principle of each of A.A.'s Twelve Steps. For without some degree of humility, no alcoholic can stay sober at all. Nearly all of A.A.'s have found, too, that unless they develop much more of this precious quality than may be required just for sobriety, they still haven't much chance of becoming truly happy. Without it, they cannot live to much useful purpose, or, in adversity, be able to summon the faith that can meet any emergency.

Now this is real. This is true. Wherever I go, whatever I have to do, my heavenly Father will take care of me. No harm will come to me. This is because of a relationship with God, I thank God, I praise God, I acknowledge God's presence. I am only here today but for the grace of God.

At one time, I always wanted credit. I wanted acknowledgment. I wanted a pat on the back. No matter what I did, or for whom, it didn't make no difference. Whether it was my wife or anybody else, it didn't make no difference. Never once did I do anything out of the kindness of my heart. My attitude toward life is stingy. I'm selfish. My attitude is that I did my job. Now it's your turn to do your job. I'm supposed to do this and not that, I don't have to do that anymore. Now that's a heck of life. We talked about this way of life in Step One. This is a way of life that we were talking about in Step One. It's an unmanageable life. Here I am, sober, and my life is still unmanageable. As soon as I step into the picture, I'm in trouble again. I'm pushing and shoving. I'm saying this, and I'm saying that.

I don't want to look at these things. I want to walk right past them. God will give me an idea, an intuitive thought and I'll say, "No, I don't want to do that." He'll put a homeless person in front of me who hits me up for money and I'll say, "No, I'm not going to give him no money. Let him go out and get a job on his own." Look at me. Here in the day I'm in, I'll be in a car that I own, with some money in my pocket, and I can't give a guy an extra buck. Now my God says, "Here I'm going to show you something that will make you a better person." So I started to wonder what would happen if I gave him a buck. What would that do for me? Well, it might give me peace of mind. It might give me a sense of gratitude. It might give my mind some sense of the good world I'm in. It's not about the other person at all. I don't know what a buck will do for this street person, but I know what it will do for me. It'll make my mind mellower, softer. I won't have to walk around later wishing I had given him something. That's what I generally do: kick myself in the hind end for not doing something God told me to do.

This is a great life. This is a beautiful life when it's guided by the character God says I can be. Page 71 of the Twelve by Twelve says:

> In all these strivings, so many of them well-intentioned, our crippling handicap had been our lack of humility. We had lacked the perspective to see that character-building and spiritual values had to come first, and that material satisfactions were not the purpose of living. Quite characteristically, we had gone all out in confusing the ends with the means. Instead of regarding the satisfaction of our material desires as the means by which we could live and function as human beings, we had taken these satisfactions to be the final end and aim of life.

Well, that's what I did, too. When I got sober, I went to work, saved money, bought a new house, two-hundred-dollar suits. Back in 1954, a two-hundred-dollar suit was a really nice suit. Then I got a motorhome, a motorcycle, dune buggies. I used to race out on the desert all the time. I used to water ski. I was a jumper and a slalom guy. I was living high on the hog, but my mind was no good. I was angry. I was impatient. I was intolerant. I'd put my boat on a ramp, and I'd say to anybody who got in my way, "Get the heck out of the way and let me get my boat down there." If somebody went by me in their boat, I'd say, "Don't go by me so fast. Don't make the water so rough."

Now I know that I don't have to go out into the world and live like that. I don't have to act like a jerk. I've experienced all the things I'm talking about. This isn't something I've read. This doesn't come from any of the babies I've worked with or from my sponsor. This comes from my own life. So why not take advantage of my life? On page 59 of the Twelve by Twelve, in reference to the Fifth Step, its says that I had to have the help of God and another human being. So what does that mean? It means that we're here to help each other. Like my sponsor said, "I'm going to take the bumps out of the road for you." This is not a trial-and-error program. This is a sure-fire hit, every time. My sponsor said, "You listen carefully. I'm going to give you everything I've got to help you in your life so that you can go farther with what you have." That's exactly what the Big Book means on page 17 when it refers to "brotherly and harmonious action." You don't have to go through a period of trial and error or go through a period of maybe five years and then find out that you could have done something different to make your recovery go faster. You have a good wife. You have a good job. You have whatever. Why should you have to lose it all and struggle to find it again? Why not find what you need now? Why not use this program of recovery instead of saying, "Naw, I don't want that. I don't want to use that." This was the attitude I had all the time. I thought for sure that everything I was being asked to do made me less of a man, and it was exactly the opposite. It made me a better man. It made the world I live in a good world.

There's a lot to talk about in Step Seven. On page 72 of the Twelve by Twelve, it says:

> We never thought of making honesty, tolerance, and true love of man and God the daily basis of living.
>
> This lack of anchorage to any permanent values, this blindness to the true purpose of our lives produced another bad result. For as long as we were convinced that we could live exclusively by our own individual strength and intelligence, for just that long was a working faith in a Higher Power impossible. This was true even when we believed that God existed. We could actually have earnest religious beliefs which remained barren because we were still trying to play God ourselves. As long as we placed self-reliance first, a genuine reliance upon a Higher Power was out of the

> question. That basic ingredient of all humility, a desire to seek and do God's will, was missing.

Now what does this mean? Again on page 72, it says:

> For us, the process of gaining a new perspective was unbelievably painful. It was only by repeated humiliations that we were forced to learn something about humility. It was only at the end of a long road, marked by successive defeats and humiliations, and the final crushing of our self-sufficiency, that we began to feel humility as something more than groveling despair. Every newcomer in Alcoholics Anonymous is told, and soon realizes for himself, that his humble admission of powerlessness over alcohol is the first step toward liberation from its paralyzing grip.

I had to learn that humility is all about doing something because I need to do it. It means giving of self. It means that I'm not first, now, in the life that I'm in. You're first. I have to consider you. I used to live in an empty world, a world of my own. I did as I pleased, without considering you or your needs. I was a hermit living in a cave, doing as I pleased because no one else was around.

Well, here I am now, in another world. I'm in a world with other people. I am responsible for how I act toward them and what I say to them. This is not for these other people; it's for me. I'm not behaving differently to please them. I'm doing it because this is going to make me, in the day I'm in, somebody by the power of God. God says, "I'll show you how to act here, but you have to do as I say, not as you say." This is what Step Seven is about. Humility and humbleness means there is less self in my life. Today I give God credit for everything in my life.

A long time ago, when I was Twelve Stepping, I'd put guys in hotels. I'd spend my own money. I'd do things, but I did it because I wanted to blow my horn. I'd go back to meetings, and I'd tell the guys in the meetings about all my good works, about how I helped this guy and that guy, how much money I spent, and whatever else I was doing. And they'd tell me, "Bob, you better go out and do it again because you didn't get no credit for it the first time. That horn you blew is the only recognition you'll ever get. Why don't you keep your mouth shut?" This is the way they used to talk to me. They'd say, "Why don't you go out and help somebody and don't tell anybody about it? Then maybe God will help you." This is what Step Seven is all about. On page 74 of the Twelve by Twelve, it says:

> But when we have taken a square look at some of these defects, have discussed them with another, and have become willing to have them removed, our thinking about humility c ommences to have a wider meaning. By this time in all probability we have gained some measure of release from our more devastating handicaps. We enjoy moments in which there is something like real peace of mind. To those of us who have hitherto known only excitement, depression, or anxiety—in other words, to all of u—this newfound peace is a priceless gift. Something new, indeed, has been added. Where humility had formerly stood for forced feeding on humble pie, it now begins to mean the nourishing ingredient which can give us serenity.

Now remember, I have been trying to apply the Steps so that my character can change. When the Twelve by Twelve says "we have taken a square look at these defects," it's talking about Step Four. When it says we "have discussed them with another," it's referring to Step Five. When it says we "have become willing to have them removed," it's referring to Step Six. When it says that "our thinking about humility commences to have a wider meaning," it's talking about a program of recovery that becomes a way of life. A program of recovery isn't about "reading" because, when you close the book, your reading is done. A program of recovery is about building a new character by applying the Steps so that I can have, today, exactly what God intends for me. This is a program of recovery. But it's not a program of recovery from yesterday. And it's not a program of recovery for tomorrow. It's a program of recovery in which I, the character I am today, do the things I need to do today. It's about staying with the power of God today instead of staying with alcoholism and yesterdays.

What qualifies us to be a part of this recovery process? The disease of alcoholism. That's it. You can be big or small, dumb or smart, rich or poor, black or white. It doesn't make no difference. If you have the disease of alcoholism, you are qualified to have something you could never have before. This new way of life, today, this day. On page 75 of the Twelve by Twelve, it says:

> During this process of learning more about humility, the most profound result of all was the change in our attitude toward God. And this was true whether we had been believers or unbelievers. We began to get over the idea that the Higher Power was a sort of bush-league pinch hitter, to be called upon only in an emergency. The notion that we would still live our own lives, God helping a little now and then, began to evaporate. Many of us who had thought ourselves religious awoke to the limitations of this attitude. Refusing to place God first, we had deprived ourselves of His help. But now the words "Of myself I am nothing, the Father doeth the works" began to carry bright promise and meaning.

They're telling me something here that I need, today. This isn't about reading something, saying, "Boy, I agree with that," and then moving on. This is a textbook for living. I had to get over the idea that God "was a sort of bush-league pinch hitter." God wasn't in my life at all when I was drinking. When I came to this program, I found God but I said, "God, I need your help here" or "God, I need your help there." I thought of God only when I was in trouble. Now these words say that recovery requires something different.

In Step Three, I made a decision to turn my will and my life over to the care of God *as I understood him*. From that moment on, God's power is in my life and I can do Step Four. Now when I do one Step, I don't leave it behind. I didn't do Step Four by leaving God back in Step Three. I didn't do Step Five by leaving my inventory back in Step Four. I have to take these Steps with me. I have to draw from them. I have to use them. They have to be with me.

I couldn't get this concept for a long time. I kept losing it. I'd get down the line and one angry thought would put me right back in the disease. One hundred percent. The program of recovery shows me that I don't have to flip-flop. It gives me something with which I can start walking and talking. God-consciousness can start to be in my mind.

A long time ago, I thought this was like religion, like dogma, like ritual, with buildings and kneeling and praying and all that. But it isn't like that. This isn't about praying. This is about living in the world today with a power behind me that is not me. I'll tell you what, this was difficult for me to understand. I couldn't get it through my brain because I'm always in there, figuring out life, thinking in terms of me doing this and me doing that. But it isn't about me doing this or me doing that. It's about God doing it. And it's not about turning God on and off. You can say, "God, help me here," and then leave God out of the picture once you get what you need. And when you get in trouble again, you say "Help me" again. But that's not what this program of recovery is about. God can help you all the time if you have a God-consciousness. Why do you have to get in trouble before you call on him? I'm not preaching to you. This is a message that I need to hear. I can't live on yesterday's sobriety, yesterday's happiness, yesterday's prayers. The only way I can be somebody today is through the power of God. This is not a self-help program. This is strictly a God-help program for now, this time, right now.

Step Seven is where I had a breakthrough. I found a way of life in Step Seven and it was all about that toothpick on the floor. Picking up that toothpick is the same thing as doing something in your own house that you normally think is not your job. I used to come home from work with the attitude that I already did what I was supposed to do, just by going to work. Oh, I might cut the grass because I figured that was my job but I wouldn't do the dishes because I figured that was her job. At some point, when I noticed the dishes needed to be done, I did them. I didn't do them to get an acknowledgment, a pat on the back, or a return on my favor. I recognized that I could do things that would add to my life. I learned to go a little farther than I would normally go. And I learned that it helped me. Now I do all kinds of things because I feel good after I do them. Things like holding a door open. You hold a door open because you see somebody coming. You could pretend that you don't see them and keep on going. That's what I used to do. Today I'll hold the door open because I've learned that these little things can make my life beautiful. I can live in a different world when I do things that others appreciate. When I'm in the program of recovery, I have a good life. People want to be around me. This is what Step Seven is about. With humility and humbleness, I can recognize that life is full of good things to do and that I can contribute to this world. At one time, I used to skip over the little things. I thought they were unimportant. Now I recognize that whatever I do, no matter how small, involves somebody else. Maybe I can add a little pleasure to their lives, maybe take a load off them, maybe help them in some way. But, in turn, it helps me a great deal.

This way of giving started with a toothpick on the floor and has turned into a lot of things.

My life is getting better and better. It blows me away. When God does something for me, I think it couldn't get any better. But then the next day comes and God outdoes the day before. This is a spiritual life. It's a growing spiritual life.

The Twelve by Twelve, referring to Step Six, says on page 64:

> Having been granted a perfect release from alcoholism, why then shouldn't we be able to achieve by the same means a perfect release from every other difficulty or defect? This is the riddle of existence ....

Now on page 74 it says the same thing, in different words, about Step Seven:

> The Seventh Step is where we make a change in our attitude which permits us, with humility as our guide, to move out from ourselves towards others and towards God. The whole emphasis of Step Seven is on humility. It is really saying to us that we now ought to be willing to try humility in seeking the removal of our shortcomings just as we did when we admitted we were powerless over alcohol, and came to believe that a power greater than ourselves could restore us to sanity. If that degree of humility could enable us to find the grace by which such a deadly obsession could be banished, then there must be hope of the same results respecting any other problem we possibly could have.

The two statements are the same. This life is a growing life, a continuous life, a good life. At one time, in my alcoholism, I couldn't get rid of the disease. It was killing me. All of sudden, God took my alcoholism right out of my life. Just like that. The only thing I did was come to this program. I did not pray, but I did not get drunk because God still looked after me. I've gone right up until now, and I still haven't gotten drunk. So God did something for me, just as the literature said he would. He's proceeded to do exactly what was promised. Here in Step Seven, it says that if he can remove my alcoholism, why can't he remove any other difficulty or defect? God can do anything. But first I had to learn that humility and humbleness are the principles I needed to live by. All of us have to discover this and make it a way of life. Step Seven is where I, myself, found peace of mind. I found many other wonderful things in my life because of Step Seven. It made me a giver, not a taker. Now, through Step Seven, I have to be a giver all the time. Never a taker.

Here are some questions I've been asked about this Step.

▲ I sometimes think that the principles that come out of Step Seven sum up the character I should be in sobriety. Is there any truth to this statement?

Absolutely. On page 71 of the Twelve by Twelve, it says:

> True, most of us thought good character was desirable, but obviously good character was something one needed to get on with the business of being self-satisfied. With a proper display of honesty and morality, we'd stand a better chance of getting what we really wanted. But whenever we had to choose between character and comfort, the character building was lost in the dust of our chase after what we thought was happiness. Seldom did we look at character building as something desirable in itself, something we would like to strive for whether our instinctual needs were met or not. We never thought of making honesty, tolerance, and true love of man and God the daily basis of living.

The phrase "character building" occurs throughout the literature's discussion of the Steps. Moreover, the Twelve by Twelve tells you on every page what to do and what not to do. There is a formula. There is a method. This is a way of life, no matter how you look at it. Every one of us is guaranteed that this method will do what it is supposed to do. It'll take care of our alcoholism.

This Step made the word "character" acceptable for me. I kept hearing the word, "character," over and over again.

And I didn't like it. Now, through this Step, I want to build a new character. I want to know more about this character, what this character needs, how to identify this character. I never expected this program to turn into a twenty-four-hour-a-day way of life. I never thought that this new character would go with me wherever I went. Nor did I know that the disease of alcoholism, if it isn't treated, will stay with me wherever I go. If you think you're safe and secure just because you go to a lot of meetings and have a lot of years, think again. You walk out into that world and call upon your own brains and, bang, it happens. You're right back where you started. And so you're asking yourself, "Don't all those meetings count?" No, they don't count. "Doesn't my reading count?" No, it doesn't count either. The only thing that counts is your relationship with God and whether you've adopted a method of living based on living with his power. That's what counts.

At one time, I used to wonder if I was going to do anything besides talk about God and the Steps. But really that's all there is. That's all that's needed. That's where the good life is. That's where all the happiness, all of the well-being, all of the everything for my life today is. I appreciate it. I know it. I feel it. The guys I hang around with know it. Their lives keep getting better and better all the time. There's no money that can buy the way of life I have today. And I wouldn't trade it for nothing else. Why should I? This happiness isn't found outside of me. Happiness is inside me. My accomplishments and possessions are nice to have and I love them, but my happiness isn't found in those things. My happiness is right here, right now.

▲ I practice Step Seven a lot. Not because I truly want to but because I know I'll die if I don't. Am I missing the mark by practicing this Step because I have to instead of because I want to?

In a sense, yes. I had to find this out for myself, but I did get some help from Dr. Tiebout in *Surrender vs. Compliance*. I do things for different reasons. I do some things for favors. I do some things under protest. I do some things to gain something. So I had to learn the difference between "compliance" and "surrender." Now this word "surrender" is a big word but it's an important part of the program. I didn't know the meaning of the word when I first got to the program. I thought it was about giving up. If you're getting whipped, you better surrender. You better quit. So I thought surrendering meant quitting. Surrendering in that sense just left me high and dry, with nothing. It meant I ended something. That's all.

Now, in the sense that the program uses the word, surrendering is an ending but it's also a beginning. Surrendering is about ending your old self and beginning a new self, a new program of recovery, a new character. You end the old way of life, the old way of thinking, acting, being, and you begin a new way of life. Before the program, I associated surrendering with having a yellow streak. If you surrendered, I thought you were less of a man. So I thought, "I'll never surrender. I'm not going to give this up. I'll make it work some way."

Well, then I got to the point where I would do it but under protest. In other words, I complied. I didn't want to do what the program told me to do, but I had to do it. I did it but I felt like you made me do it. So you forced me into doing something right, but me and my character didn't really change. I was still the old character.

I found out through Dr. Tiebout that if I comply, I'm not surrendering. And I need to surrender to really change. So compliance gets in my way, compliance stops me from surrendering and really changing. Compliance lets me go ahead and do my own thing. As Dr. Tiebout says:

> It is now possible to link compliance with the problem of alcoholism and also to the theory of surrender. The link between alcoholism and compliance has already been shown in the alcoholic's repeated vows that he would never take another drink, vows which go by the board because of of the inner ability to do no more than comply. The presence of a strong vein of unconscious compliance in the alcoholic can be demonstrated in other ways. Alcoholics are a notably pleasant and agreeable group with a marked tendency to say "yes" when approached directly. They claim they want to be well liked—hence their willingness to promise anything. Yet—the other side of the compliance reaction is manifest—they balk at the showdown and are ever likely to renege on their original promises. As another illustration, they are keen to go to a show, buy tickets in advance, and then on the night of the performance wish they had never had the idea.

Surrender is at the heart of Step Seven. If you're not surrendered, you have not applied the Step.

Without Step Seven, I would have to stay exactly where I was in Step Six. In Step Six, I was entirely ready to have God remove all these defects of character. Without Step Seven, I would be left empty. Step Seven is where I begin to live in the world I'm in. Step Seven is where my disease starts getting treated. Steps One to Six are not about treating my disease. They are about finding out what's wrong with me and what's needed to treat my disease. This is totally different from Steps Seven through Twelve. Start looking at Steps One through Twelve for what they really say and what they really do. Steps One through Six are always about me, the disease, and what's needed to treat the disease. These Steps are always about what's wrong, what I did, why my life's unmanageable and so on. Without Step Seven, I'd be stuck. Step Seven is where I start to live. I start to appreciate life. I start to think a lot of me because of what I'm doing. I start looking inside me and I realize I'm not a bad guy after all.

Moreover, if I didn't do Step Seven, I couldn't do the Steps that follow. I couldn't make a list of the people I had harmed and couldn't make amends to them because I'd still be all wrapped up in me. Step Seven says, "Let's stop thinking about ourselves. Let's start thinking about God and other people. Let's start doing something now. Let's start giving. Give of your heart, your soul, your money, your mind, your whole being. It's possible for me to do this now because there is something that I believe in. That's God first, not me. God gets credit. Not me. Humility and humbleness isn't about giving myself credit. It's about doing things because God says I should do them. This is what sets me free. Free of self. Free of the bondage of self. Free of the old life. Free of alcoholic thinking, acting, being. Step Seven is where I get reborn. I get reborn because of an application that starts in Step Seven, not in Step Three. Step Three is where the freedom is identified as being relieved of the bondage of self through the power of God. Step Seven is where the power of God enters my life, where I learn to live in this power, and begin to express his will. Now I'm doing his works. His works. This is what I pray about all the time. Step Seven is where God gets the credit and He gives me the power.

On Step Eight

Becoming Willing

Made a list of all persons I had harmed and became willing to make amends to them all.*

Based on what I've found myself and what I've learned through the years from working with others, the next two Steps aren't too difficult and they don't need a drawn-out explanation.

To start off, with regard to character building, there is something brought to Step Eight from Step Four. In Step Four, I discovered many defects of character in myself. Now these defects of character, which involved my relationships with others, are the basis of Step Eight. We'll get back to that.

In the alcoholism stage, I was the kind of man who harmed anybody who came into my life. I took advantage of situations and people: my family, my mother, my father, my brothers, my sisters, my boss, and the guys I worked with—at least, the guys who would let me get away with things.

Before I got here, I never realized the meaning of the word "harm." I didn't think that certain things were harmful. As far as I was concerned, I associated harm only with the things I did when I was drunk. That's the only harm I knew. When I

*For the sake of my own recovery, I changed the Steps to first-person singular.

got into this recovery program, I learned to look at my track record, up to the present, whether I was drunk or sober. Not only do I have to clear away the wreckage of the past, which is to say the harm I did in my life as a drunk, but I had to learn to live today so that I don't create a wreckage of the present in my sober life. It's the same story I've told before. The harm that I used to do could still be with me today because I still think and act the same. The new character that I'm building isn't here to clear away just the wreckage of the past. In other words, character building isn't about straightening out some things so that you can go along and do as you please. I have to clear away the wreckage of the past so that I don't repeat the wreckage and fall into living my life the old way.

On page 80 of the Twelve by Twelve, it says:

> We might ask ourselves what we mean when we say that we have "harmed" other people. What kind of "harm" do people do to one another anyway? To define the word "harm" in a practical way, we might call it the result of instincts in collision, which cause physical, mental, emotional, or spiritual damage to people.

Now this was too obvious to be useful to me. I had to go onto page 81:

> Such gross behavior is not by any means a full catalog of harms we do. Let us think of some of the subtler ones which can sometimes be quite as damaging. Suppose that in our family lives we happen to be miserly, irresponsible, callous, cold. Suppose that we are irritable, critical, impatient, humorless. Suppose we lavish attention upon one member of the family and neglect the others. What happens when we try to dominate the whole family, either by a rule of iron or by a constant outpouring of minute directions for just how their life should be lived from hour to hour? What happens when

> we wallow in depression, self-pity oozing from every pore, and inflict that upon those about us? Such a roster of harms done to others, the kind that makes daily living with us as practicing alcoholics difficult and often unbearable, could be extended almost indefinitely. When we take personality traits such as these into shop, office, and the society of our fellows, they can do damage almost as extensive as that we have caused at home.

Now these were the harms that I didn't know about. These were the harms that I had to find out about in myself. Now I knew about the obvious harms. Maybe I'd smash somebody's car or their property. Maybe I stole from somebody. Maybe I abused somebody. But I had never thought about the harms written on page 81. Here I had a chance to think about the harm caused by my moods. I had mood swings. I have a mind that gets upset, that gets angry, and it just hates everybody. I'll even hurt my closest friend, the one I love the most.

This helped me think about all the people I had harmed in this way. I thought about all these situations where I had taken advantage of my father and my sister and so on. And I realized these were things I had to do something about. So I started to make a list of all the people I had harmed. Now I didn't know what to say to them yet, but I could write their names down and I could realize that I was willing to make amends. Even if I didn't know, right then, how to do it.

▲ I've stolen from so many people, going so far back, that this Step overwhelms me. I get all caught up into all this money I owe. So I tried to make it simple by focusing on the people in my life now and making amends to them.

Step Eight is where you make a list of the people you've harmed. Step Nine is where you make the direct amends to those people wherever possible. In Step Eight, the only thing you have to do is to recognize or identify the harms that you're talking about. See, Step Eight is a little bit different from Step Nine. Okay, you haven't been able to do Step Eight yet. You're afraid to make the list. That's what you should look at—why you're afraid to make the list. Making the list is not the same as making amends. All it means is that you identify the people you need to make amends to.

Then you need to become *willing* to make amends to them. So then you might have to look at why you don't have the willingness to make amends to them. Maybe you're scared of the contact. Maybe you don't want to part with the money. That's what you have to look at in this Step.

▲ I think that if I make the list, then I have to go ahead and make the amends.

You sure do. If you make the list, you'll have to go on to Step Nine and make the amends. This is a program of recovery. But making the amends is Step Nine, not Step Eight.

▲ I ripped off this company. They called me, and I had to sign these papers admitting that I stole from them. Was that an amends? Do I need to make further amends to them?

So you're saying signing a piece of paper gets you off the hook? You don't have to do anything? I'll tell you what. This is a program of self-honesty. It's not a program of honesty to your neighbor. You're not here to examine somebody else's life. You're here for your own life. And if you don't want to benefit from this program, you can remain the same as you've always been and leave your alcoholism untreated.

▲ I just finished my Eighth Step before coming here, and my sponsor told me to get my list together and do the Ninth Step. Now most of my list came out of my Fourth Step. But now I'm thinking of people and incidents that didn't come up in my Fourth Step. Do I put them on my list anyway and go on and make amends to them or do I have to go back to the Fourth Step?

You've noticed that the Eighth Step is related to doing an inventory. Now the Big Book talks about how you can do an annual or a semi-annual inventory. I've known some guys who do inventories more often. Of course, you do a daily inventory in Step Ten, but we're not there yet. So we have to look at what it says in Step Eight and it says: I have to make a list of all those I have harmed and become willing to make amends to them all. You can't eliminate this Step, but it is not such a huge Step and you don't have to talk about it for centuries. Sure, Step Four is a good basis for making this list. Like you, I found that Step Four can be found in Step Eight. But you don't have to do any more than what it says: You make a list of all persons you have harmed and become willing to make amends to them all.

Now, I don't think this should be too overwhelming. I'm sure there are people from your past that you have harmed. You can write their names down, and you can write them down very clearly. I know you can do it. I'm not saying you want to do it. I'm saying you can do it. You can do it because you've worked the seven Steps that went before. Now if I haven't done the first seven Steps, I'm probably not going to be able to do this Step yet. But if I've done the Steps before, then I can do this. It's a guarantee.

On Step Nine

Clearing Away the Wreckage Of the Past and Present

Made direct amends to such people wherever possible, except when to do so would injure them or others.*

I don't think that talking about Step Nine is a big deal. However, there are some important things to recognize.

It says in the literature—and I know this is true—that there are certain amends that I can never make. I can't make amends at somebody else's expense. I can't go out and make amends to those I have harmed when to do so would cause more harm or a bunch of grief. I can't use this Step for my own advantage and wind up hurting people. I think it's obvious what this means. Generally, when this comes up, sex is involved or something from our drunken past. I don't think this is a big issue myself.

Each one of us has a record for which we can make amends. To make a list of all the persons I had harmed—that wasn't very hard to do. But I had to learn how to make amends. When I made my list, I realized I had to make amends to my father. I flew back East to see him. He told me, "No, you don't have to make amends to me. Just stay with those people you are with." And I told him, "No, that's

*For the sake of my own recovery, I changed the Steps to first-person singular.

not good enough. I have to tell you exactly what happened, what I did, and how sorry I am that I behaved that way." So I explained to him that I was drunk. That I was out of my mind. That I couldn't always recall what I did, but I knew that at least I could apologize for whatever it was. And that was the end of that one. Now that was the hardest one for me—because I had beaten up my old man. I beat him up bad. After I did that, I suffered for it. I suffered for it when I was drunk. I suffered for it when I was sober. But when it came time to tell him about it, the telling did exactly what it was supposed to do. It removed this incident from my mind as hurt. It removed it from my mind as a memory that would make me sick.

You have to make your own list. How you go about making amends for yourself, I don't know. One thing for sure I know: A lot of people don't want to speak to the people they hurt. But you have to in many instances because this is the only way you can clear away the wreckage of the past. I had to tell the people on my list that things happened because of the condition of my mind when I was drunk. I would do anything to anybody and not worry about the consequences. I didn't do it because I was drunk. I did it because I did it. I did it because my mind was sick, and all I wanted was forgiveness. And that's something my father did for me.

Steps Eight and Nine are not that hard to do. I know some of you will have questions about whether you should make direct amends to somebody in your life. But I think that the Steps make clear when you need to do that. When I made up my list of all persons I had harmed and I started to write down the way I had mistreated them, I realized in many cases what I had to do. For example, I stole from people. I stole from my mother. I took her money. So I had to acknowledge these things and pay them back—directly if it was possible.

▲ How do you go about making financial amends when you don't have the money?

Willingness is what is necessary. When you have the willingness, something can always be done. Maybe you have to do it in payments. Maybe you have to do it by working for the person you have harmed. There's always a way if you're willing. As far as money goes, I didn't owe too much. I owed enough to make my life tough. I owed the IRS. But I didn't owe as much as some of the guys I know. They owed some big money. I've often wondered how you could pay back five hundred thousand dollars. But it comes up for people and if you're willing, you can find a way to take care of it.

▲ I tried to make amends to my Dad, but he wouldn't let me say what I wanted to say. He knew what I was trying to say, but he just stopped me. Just as in your situation, he told me to just keep doing what I was doing. I never had a chance to tell him why I was making amends. Should I go back?

I would. Yes, I would. The reason is that this is a program of recovery for *you*. You have to look at it this way. When my father tried to stop me from talking, I told him, "Look, this has gotta be this way. I have to do this. I need to do it for me." If I didn't do this, this stuff was going to stay inside me and eat me up. I had to tell him what I did. I had to tell him I was sorry and that I wanted to make it up to him. So, yeah, if I were you, I would sit my father down and make him listen.

▲ How do you make amends to someone who has died?

I don't really know what to tell you. You know I lost my wife, but there is no way I can write a letter and put it on her grave. No way. I know what I did. I know what I was when I was living with her. The only forgiveness I got—and this took me two years—was that I realized I could be with God and not be that way again. When I realized I didn't have to live the way I used to, that I didn't have to hurt people the way I hurt her, then I felt some forgiveness.

If you've got somebody special in your life, why don't you tell them today how important they are to you? Why don't you give them flowers? Why don't you do it today? Life is real short. If you don't want to, you don't have to. It's up to you.

▲ I have people in my life that I'd like to make direct amends to, but doing so would injure them or others. What I hear you saying is that I should make my amends to the people living in my life right now.

Absolutely. You have to recognize the people that are in your life right now. Now these could be strangers or they could be people you're close to. Even if you smile at them, that's something.

▲ Should we put ourselves on the amends list each year? If so, what was your Ninth Step like in this respect?

You know, this is a good question. There's no way that I could put myself on the list and forgive myself and make things all right. It isn't enough for me to forgive myself or to think that I can somehow help myself by doing that. I have to do something different. I have to be the man I should be in the day I'm in according to the Twelve Steps. I have to change. So I have to put other people down on the list and then make amends to them all. Not to myself. The only way I can stop hurting is to become the new character. That's the only way. I can't make amends to myself. Self doesn't have the power to forgive self. It just doesn't work that way.

▲ I'm having trouble with the phrase "except when to do so would injure them or others."

This means that I can't get rid of something if somebody is going to get hurt in the process. A lot of things that we might want to bring out into the open again would hurt somebody. You have to pay the price yourself, or you can't do it.

▲ Can you expound on the idea of making "direct amends"? As part of my Ninth Step, I went to my wife and said I was sorry. Now this made me feel better, but it seemed to depress her and it didn't seem to be as important as what I did to change my behavior. I never went to my parents and said I was sorry for things I had done, but I did a lot of things that changed my behavior with regard to them. When you make amends, do you have to go to someone and say you are sorry?

I made amends to everyone I could think of, except my wife. To make amends, I had to learn to go talk to them first, to tell them what I'm doing and why. I had to explain to them that I acted the way I did because I had no choice. I was an alcoholic. I went back to Cleveland and talked to my father and explained to him why I had to make amends to him. He tried to stop me by saying, "Just stay with the people you're with, and that's amends enough for me." But I said: "No, that's not the way it works." I told him I acted badly and that what I did was going to stay in me until I was released from it. I had to tell him exactly what happened and how I felt about it. So I did. I told him exactly what happened, how I lived, how I thought, and what I did to hurt him. I hurt him real bad. I hurt him severely, physically. And I told him I had to bring this out in the open and genuinely ask his forgiveness for what I did.

Whether or not he could give me that forgiveness was not important. That wasn't why I was there. I was not there so I would become all right when he forgave me. I had to do what

I did, I had to tell him everything, so that I would know what was wrong with me and what I did. I had to be genuine. I had to be the true character that I am. I did this so I could be who I should be. When I admit what I did and who I was, I release myself from having to live like that again or having to treat anybody, including him, like that again.

This step isn't about just to go to somebody and say I'm sorry. That doesn't work. That will never work. I'll just turn right around and I'll act in the same way or worse to somebody else down the line. And I can't blame it on alcohol because I'm doing it sober. I'm doing it in the program. I'm not the man I say I am. I'm not full of forgiveness. I'm not.

The purpose of the Ninth Step is character building. So I have to do the Ninth Step the way it should be done. Not to get past something or to get off the hook. Not to sluff through it or say, "Man, I did it, I'm glad that's over with." That's baloney. I went to my mother, my father, my brothers, my sisters, and I went to others around me, different ones. The reason I talked to them was not to get off the hook but to be able to look at myself and realize that God just did something for me to be relieved of the bondage of self. I needed to be able to reach inside and know that I was genuinely sorry that I harmed this world and that I didn't ever want to do that again.

I can get forgiveness from God. I can't get the person I hurt to forgive me. They might say the words. They might say it's okay. Whatever they say, that isn't what I'm looking for. I don't want that. I don't need that. But I want the relationship with God. I want to have the clean mind. I don't want to go on memory, memory, memory. Memory can kill you. If you don't do something about it, you walk around with stuff that's killing you. Every time a name comes up. Every time maybe you hear a song. Every time you read or look at a letter. Here comes a bunch of crap with it. You know what that crap's from? From the yesteryears that you never cleaned up. You never looked at. You're still living in the mind of yesteryear.

Part 5

Happily and Usefully Whole In Each Day You Live

On Step Ten

Continue to Look Inwardly Today

Continued to take personal inventory and when I was wrong promptly admitted it.*

Taking a personal inventory means that you look inwardly in the day you're in. On page 12 of the Twelve by Twelve, it says:

> A spotcheck inventory taken in the midst of such disturbances can be of great help in quieting stormy emotions. Today's spotcheck finds its chief application to situations which arise in each day's march. The consideration of longstanding difficulties had better be postponed, when possible, to times deliberately set aside for the purpose. The quick inventory is aimed at our daily ups and downs, especially those where people or new events throw us off balance and tempt us to make mistakes.

My sponsor said the same thing. He said Step Ten is going to allow me to live in this day, today, without acquiring new defects of character, without making mistakes and then lugging these mistakes around with me all day. I don't have to

*For the sake of my own recovery, I changed the Steps to first-person singular.

create a life full of me and mistakes and then wait until I get home at night and pray to God, on my knees, for forgiveness. He said, "No, it don't work that way." Step Ten means exactly what it says: to promptly admit when I am wrong.

To whom do I promptly admit my wrongs? To a power greater than myself, to God. When do I admit to God my wrongs? The minute I do them. Why is it like this? Because the moment I recognize the wrong, the moment I identify the wrong, I must do something.

If I make a mistake or am about to make a mistake, I have the ability to promptly admit it. I can ask for help. I don't have to go farther with the mistake. I can stop what I'm doing and I can be forgiven, instantly, for what I did. I don't have to build a case against myself or anyone else.

Otherwise, I keep adding to my woes. I compound things and carry them with me. For instance, if I do something wrong, small or big, at eleven o'clock in the morning and carry it with me, I start compounding things. In other words, if I make a mistake and don't do anything about it, I'll do something else. Here I am, in the day I'm in, starting to get loaded with mistakes that are going to kill me.

There's no reason why any of us can't, in the day we're in, make a mistake and get it corrected immediately. But you can only get a mistake corrected through the grace of God, by identifying to God that you need help, that you did something you wish you hadn't done. I do this all the time. I'm always asking God for forgiveness. "I'm sorry. I did it again. Would you help me?" I don't have to stay where I'm at, get upset, or kick myself in the hind end and feel guilty all day. Step Ten says you don't have to live like that. On page 90, the Twelve by Twelve says: "It's a spiritual axiom that every time I am disturbed, no matter what the cause, there is something wrong with me."

Step Ten is where I learned to take the blame even when I wasn't to blame. I say I'm wrong even when I'm right so that somebody else, anybody else, doesn't have to be loaded with, frightened by, or hurt by the wrong. I am even that way with my daughters. I can take the blame with anybody, anywhere. It could be in a market. It could be with a stranger. It could be with someone I know. I don't have to prove anything to make myself right. Why do I have to hurt somebody by proving myself right to them? I don't need to do that. My ego used to tell me to prove myself, but now I don't need to do that.

I have to practice this as a way of life today, this day. I have to build this character in my life today because this disease is never a "wasm." There's no place I can hide this disease. I have to live by this program of recovery or I don't have it. I know I'm repeating this, but it's important. You cannot shorten this thing up or bypass anything by saying that you're all right now. This is a program of recovery and to do this Step, you have to do the nine that came before it. You can't cheat.

For a long time, I wouldn't buy the idea that "whenever something disturbs me, no matter what the cause, I'm at fault." After I did buy it, after I realized that it's not important to be right or wrong, I entered a brand-new world. I no longer have to prove myself to feel better. I don't have to put you down by telling you that you're wrong. Why should I do that? If you want to think a wall is black and I think it's white, I don't care. Go ahead and think it's black. What you think won't hurt me. Before I used to get upset with things like that. I'd think, "He's really a dummy."

This principle applies to anything. Walls, someone else's behavior, someone's driving. Anything. You name it. The way you look no longer makes any difference to me. You can be who you are and I won't want to change you. This, by the way, is the meaning behind the slogan, "Live and let live."

My old way of thinking was really destructive. The power of self does the same thing to you as it does to me. My old way of thinking made the world unmanageable. It's not the right way to think.

In Step Ten, we *promptly* admitted when we were wrong.

Promptly admitted. This means we admit the wrong to God now. I know I've been talking about "now" since the beginning of this book, but the concept of "now" is much more pronounced in Step Ten than anywhere else. To continue to take personal inventory means I have to look inside myself, not in my past but in my present. Whatever I do, wherever I go, I must be able to do this personal inventory right now. Whatever I do, wherever I go, I have to carry the principle of Step Ten with me.

▲ The Twelve by Twelve talks about three kinds of inventories in relationship to Step Ten. One is a spotcheck. The second is a daily inventory. The third is a careful review with a sponsor. Isn't the last one closer to what is meant in the Fifth Step? And can you explain what the book means by a semi-annual or annual housecleaning?

On page 90 of the Twelve by Twelve, it says, "Although all inventories are alike in principle, a time factor does distinguish one from another." The spotcheck inventory is what I was describing above. It's something I do right at the moment you do something wrong. It's checking in with my God to see how I'm doing. The book says that the spotcheck inventory is taken any time of the day when I find myself getting tangled up. If I make a mistake, if I go somewhere I shouldn't go, I can have that mistake corrected. Instantly.

The daily inventory is similar to the inventory you take in the Fourth Step except you take it at the end of the day and review how you did that day.

On the other hand, you can do a careful review with a sponsor at any time at all. For example, when I speak to those I sponsor, they may talk about this or that or have a problem or a question. These reviews can be periodic, a daily or a nightly happening. Now on page 90, the Twelve by Twelve refers to the semi-annual or annual housecleaning. People may refer to this type of inventory as a Tenth Step rather than a Fifth Step, but it is not. The book just wants to say that you, as an alcoholic, can do a housecleaning any time you want. Maybe you did one inventory and think you should do more. There is nothing wrong with doing another housecleaning. It's up to each one of us, as individual alcoholics, to decide whether we want to get all our defects of character out at once or do an annual housecleaning. I can't tell someone, "You better take another inventory." I'm not your jury. I'm not your God. Determining whether you need another inventory is an inside job. I can present you with the food, but you're going to have to decide yourself whether to eat it. If you are willing to go to any length in your recovery, then you're going to have to take certain Steps. But I can't take the Steps for you.

▲ After you admit that you are wrong to God, do you try to make amends to the persons involved in the wrong?

Steps Eight and Nine answer this question. When I take Steps Eight and Nine the first time, I am not finished with them. The Steps are not designed just to get rid of things that happened a long time ago. The purpose of the Steps is to help you live right in the day you're in. Eliminating problems is part of the character building process, and this process is something that continues throughout your life. So, sure, you're absolutely right. After you have admitted to God that you were wrong, you can make amends to those you have harmed. You just have to understand that this means the Steps have to become a way of life for you and not just a way of eliminating problems from the past.

▲ How many times a day do you find yourself asking God for forgiveness because of negative thoughts that pop into your head?

Your relationship with God is an ongoing process, all the

time. The relationship began in Step Two and has continued up through Step Ten. But Step Two is generally where the people I work with have the most difficulty. I'll tell you why. Step Two says that I came to believe a power greater than myself could restore me to sanity. But if I can't get to where I believe in a power greater than myself, all I've got to believe in is me. And if I believe in only myself, I'm going to do the same thing I've always done. If you don't believe this, look at your own track record.

Thoughts don't just pop into your head. You are either with the power of self or you are with the power of God. So if you are having negative thoughts all the time, you have to consider that you might be living in the power of self. Meaning, that you still haven't gotten away from the power of self or been relieved from the bondage of self. You have not come to believe in a power greater than yourself. The idea is to learn where the disease is in your life right now and why you're here. Once you've done that and have come to believe in a power greater than yourself, then you can become free of self. Now, I can continue to live free of self through Step application. Remember the important thing is that I still have the disease and that I'm still here for the same reason that I had when I came into this program. I go to meetings and I go on retreats because I've still got the disease. I've still got alcoholism. I don't have "alcoholwasm." The disease, my selfish self, is always present. The moment the power of self rears its head, here comes the disease. We come here looking for a program of recovery, a new way to live. That new way to live is found in the Twelve Steps. The Twelve Steps will enable you to live free of self—happy, joyous and free, in the day you are in—only by Step application.

On Step Eleven

Growing Spiritually

Sought through prayer and meditation to improve my conscious contact with God, as I understood Him, praying only for knowledge of his will for me and the power to carry that out.*

There is no way you can read or interpret this Step to say something different than it does. It says that I sought through prayer and meditation to improve something. What am I improving? My conscious contact with God *as I understood him*.

So what does that mean? Remember how Step Two says that I came to believe in a power greater than myself that could restore me to sanity. Remember how Step Three says that I made a decision to turn my will and my life over to the care of God *as I understood him*. The word "understood" is emphasized the same way as it is in Step Eleven. In Step Two, the meaning is that I *understood* that there is a power greater than myself who can restore me to sanity. Now Step Eleven is telling me that I have to have something in my life, a conscious contact with God. Not only that, this is something I need to improve on. I have to get more of it. I have to stay with it. I have to live it.

Step Eleven is where I learned about a living God, not just

*For the sake of my own recovery, I changed the Steps to first-person singular.

a God I pray to. Now we haven't talked much about prayer yet, but there are two parts to it. The actual petition and the performance that needs to be done so the prayer can be answered. We'll need to talk, too, about what it means to meditate. But first, let's examine what it means to "improve my conscious contact" through prayer and meditation. When does this happen? When do I make this conscious contact? The answer is: now, in the present. I need God all the time. Whatever I do, wherever I go, I must go as a new character. I must live backed up by a power that's greater than me. I must live in a world today that is not my world. My world is a world that's harmful. That's a world that I create. At one time, I thought the world out there was hurting me. I found out that the world wasn't hurting me. I was hurting the world. I was doing things that I thought were right because I thought the world was wrong.

Step Eleven says that I "sought" through prayer and meditation to improve my conscious contact with God. Why does it say "sought"? What does that mean? To me, it is significant that the step says "sought" instead of "seek." To me, to "seek" means to search for something until I've found it. Once I find it, I'll quit searching for it. Because the Step says "sought," it's implying that this is something that never ends. Conscious contact is something I'm going to have to keep searching for. It's a growing thing. It's a going thing. It's a thing that progresses. I have to keep looking, searching, always. I have to keep going for it.

This is the only Step that talks about how you grow spiritually. You cannot grow spiritually by applying any other Step. This Step tells you how it's done. You "sought through prayer and meditation to improve your conscious contact with God." This is a growing contact. This is a living contact. This is a daily contact.

Now the Step says that you improve your conscious contact through prayer and meditation. Prayer is going out of self. It's reaching out to God, wanting to have something different. Meditation, on the other hand, is a growing inward, a going inward. This helps self slow down. Meditation is quieting my mind so that God can speak to me, so that God can give me new thoughts. God doesn't send telegrams. He gives me ideas. He gives me feelings. He gives me a way to go in the day I'm in to prove that He's there. This is all about the power of God.

Then the Step says that I improve my conscious contact with God *as I understood him*. This phrase takes us back to Step Two where I learned how to come to believe in a power greater than myself.

Then it says "praying only for knowledge of His will for me and the power to carry that out." Imagine that. I'm not praying for my will. God has a will for me. And I can pray to find out what that is and to receive the power to carry that out. That's why this program has the power it has. That's why this program does what it says it does. This is a program of recovery. It will treat alcoholism, and the reason is that there is a power greater than self.

This Step is where I grow spiritually. Steps One through Ten makes it possible for me to grow spiritually, because I am a character that is open-minded, that doesn't use defects that boomerang back on me, that is a giver, that develops the best possible relations with every human being and that can have my mind corrected in the moment I'm in. Now, I can grow freely, free from self. I can grow in this world and have new things. What I need is presented. The knowledge of God's will makes it possible for me to see what's presented. I improve on this relationship with God through prayer and meditation, so that I can have the knowledge of God's will supplied to me through new ideas, new intuitive thoughts, and new happenings. God presents himself to me through prayer and meditation—through my mind. I now have the knowledge of God's will and God gives me the power to carry it out. I live in a new world, full of beautiful people, beautiful things—all the time. God will present opportunities that I could never see before. These opportunities are unlimited and endless. For example, someone will be put in my life to do something for me I couldn't do for myself. Maybe this person will make a business deal happen that I could never have produced by myself. Maybe this person will take care of me through sickness, when by myself I wouldn't make it. These examples are endless.

After all of these Steps, One through Eleven, each of us will come to know that that there is something more than staying sober or going to meetings. It becomes something I want and need. When I have discipline, when I am honest with myself and with God, then I get a world that is beautiful. It becomes more beautiful all the time but only by God's grace, not mine. This growing, beautiful world is what's in Step Eleven. I cannot do this myself. I cannot even find out God's will for me by myself. I cannot even figure out what I need by myself. There are lots of things I think I need, but generally these things boomerang back on me. God does not say I need these things. They are not what God says I need. They are what I think I need. Without this program, I was always talking to myself, telling myself what I needed. I want her. I want this. I want that. Gimme this. Gimme that. Every time I got what I thought I wanted, it didn't please me. My happiness could not be found in what I wanted. I was restless, irritable, discontented. I wasn't connecting my needs to God. I wasn't connecting my needs to the program. I figured that life was a struggle. You live out in the world on your terms and life is a struggle. You win a few, and you lose a few. I used to say, "That's the way it goes, first your money and then your clothes." No, that ain't the way it goes. That's the way I went.

This is serious stuff, believe me. I've known guys and gals who came looking for recovery and wound up taking their own lives. At one time, I was puzzled by this. Here they were, guys I was close to, real close. One minute I'm talking to them, and the next day they're lying in a casket. They're dead. They killed themselves and they weren't even drunk!

I'd look at them and I'd think, "God, how can this be?" This disease is a killer. It does too much damage when it's left untreated. But for the grace of God, that could have been me in that casket. I'm not telling you this to scare you, rather to show you that Steps teach us how to live on God's terms. This way the disease can be treated.

We've been given an opportunity, every one of us in this program, to find a way of life that will enable us to walk through adversity. Even death. So what the heck? Why not live with a power that's greater than you? Why not have a way of life that will prevent you from getting so discouraged that you take a gun to your head and blow your brains out?

▲ Could you please talk about Bill Wilson's depression and its connection to his dependency?

At one time, Bill Wilson was number one. He was ahead of everybody. But he got into depression, which he talks about in *The Language of the Heart* on page 237. Here's part of it:

> Last Autumn, depression, having no really rational cause at all, almost took me to the cleaners. I began to be scared that I was in for another long chronic spell. Considering the grief I've had with depressions, it wasn't a bright prospect. I kept asking myself, "Why can't the Twelve Steps work to release depression?" By the hour I stared at St. Francis' prayer, "It's better to comfort than to be comforted." Here was the formula, all right, but why didn't it work? Suddenly I realized what the matter was. My basic flaw had always been dependence—almost absolute dependence—on people or circumstances, to supply me with prestige, security, and the like. Failing to get these things according to my perfectionist dreams and specifications, I had fought for them. And when defeat came, so did my depression. There wasn't a chance of making the outgoing love of St. Francis a workable and joyous way of life until these fatal and almost absolute dependencies were cut

> away. Because I had over the years undergone a little spiritual development, the absolute quality of these frightful dependencies had never been so starkly revealed. Reinforced by what grace I could secure in prayer, I found I had to exert every ounce of will and action to cut off those faulty emotional dependencies upon people, upon A.A., indeed, upon any set of circumstances whatsoever. Then only could I be free to love as Francis had. Emotional instinctual satisfactions, I saw, were really the extra dividends of having love, offering love, and expressing love appropriate to each relation of life. Plainly, I could not avail myself of God's love until I was able to offer it back to him by loving others as he would have me. And I couldn't possibly do that so long as I was victimized by false dependencies. For my dependency meant demand—demand for the possession and control of the people and the conditions surrounding me.

I needed to find out about this word "dependency" myself. It's one of those key words in the program, like "willingness" and "surrender" and "acceptance." Now I discovered that when I became dependent on certain things, I was wrapped up with my living and did not take care of my life. Now there's a difference between "living" and "life." They aren't the same things. Not a bit. Living is something I'm doing in the day I'm in: achieving things, getting things, being happy because I'm successful, being happy maybe because I own a little bit more than you do. I didn't even know that the character that I am does things like that. I just think this way. So I go ahead and become dependent upon being happy, or upon being successful, or upon getting something that is going to make my world right. Now when it doesn't happen for me, I get sick. I get depressed. I get worried. I start feeling bad. My life is inside me. I live in my mind. My feelings, my emotions, my thoughts, my self-esteem, my integrity are my life. I get so wrapped up in false dependencies—things outside my life—that I lose my life. So there's a difference between just living and being engaged in the life that God gave you. I had to learn the difference between these too. Bill talked about it. He wanted to control things. He wanted to have the things he thought he needed. And it made him depressed, dependent, and suicidal. Just because his mind was telling him things.

▲ You said you talked to God. Can you express how God touches you personally and spiritually?

Absolutely, I came into this program with no God and no prayers, but I had to learn how to pray. In Step Two, I learned that I have to have an open mind and I have to believe that there is a power greater than me. I had to quit looking at the world by "me" and build a relationship with God. I had to learn how to praise God, to make requests, or to talk with God right here today, now.

I don't have to get down on my knees or anything. I don't have a ritual or anything like that. The God-consciousness is the power that is in me to do what he asks in the day I'm in. Now this may sound crazy to some of you. At first, I didn't have a clue, but another man asked me, "Why don't you try my God because whatever you got isn't working."

So I did. I tried to do what he told me to do in relating to God because I was tired of my anger and hostility. I was really a mean man all the time. I had more trouble at work than anywhere else. I felt I had to do something. So I talked. I talked to a power that I called God. When I did this, I was staying away from me. I wasn't talking to me, and I wasn't the authority in my life any more.

You see, I'm a power. I don't know if you look at it this way, but I do. I am a power. And when I am a power, I talk to myself. I tell myself everything about the world and everything that's going on. I tell myself about people. I tell myself what I need and what I don't need. I have a relationship with myself. That's what kept me drunk out there. That's what made me do the things I did.

But it came to a point where I had to have something right now. I was mean and mad. And I was tired of being that way. So I asked myself: Why can't I pray to God right now? Why do I have to wait until I get home? Why can't I thank him right now? So that's what I learned to do. Now I thank God right now. I praise him for my even being here. I pray to him all the time in this way. I walk and talk with the power I call God. He is the Lord of my life. He is in all of my affairs. But the relationship does not stop with talking to God, I must recognize his presence in my life as doing everything for me. When a solution comes, or when someone is put in my life to help me, I recognize God in my life. I do not take my life for granted. I won't even take a waitress for granted. I thank God for her service. But this recognition of God's presence is not every once in a while, it's an attitude, it's a way of life. If I don't pray to God and recognize his presence, then I have me. I don't want me.

This is about building a relationship with a God who can do for me what I can't do for myself. That's the solution that the Twelve by Twelve talks about on page 25. You can't solve your problems by running back to self all the time. You can't pick and choose when and where you should act and how you should act. That's not the solution. That's the disease. So I've had to learn to not take the credit, in the day I'm in, for the good things that happen to me. If I don't give God the credit, I don't have anything. Period.

I used to think it was all luck. When I was in the Navy, I was drinking hard, riding bikes, getting in fights, the whole picture. I would get in and out of scrapes and think I was just lucky. Two days after I got out of the service, I hit a police car head on, head on, went through the windshield, and I got thirty-two stitches in my head. I had my whole head busted right open, on the side, my ear cut off at the top, and the doctor said I was lucky. But you know, today I know this didn't have anything to do with luck. My heavenly Father was protecting me, guiding me, saving me, taking care of me.

On Step Twelve

Carrying the Message

Having had a spiritual awakening as a result of these steps, I tried to carry this message to alcoholics and to practice these principles in all my affairs.*

The wording of this Step is important. "Having had a spiritual awakening as a result of these Steps. . . ." What Steps? Not the Twelve Steps but the eleven Steps that went before. Here I am now. I've built a character. I've had a spiritual awakening because of what happened when I applied these Steps. Now Step Eleven is where this spiritual awakening becomes really pronounced. It's the only Step that you can grow spiritually. You improve your conscious contact with prayer and meditation. Now, having had a spiritual awakening as a result of these Steps, I tried to carry "this message." Note that I'm not carrying "my message." I'm carrying "this message." It's not my message. It's not your message. It's God's message. It's already in print, and it does the same thing for every one of us. We have Twelve Steps to apply, in the day we're in, so that our disease can be treated and we can build this new character.

I know I'm repeating myself, but this disease is so strong, so devastating, so powerful, that I can say something and your

*For the sake of my own recovery, I changed the Steps to first-person singular.

ears will listen but you won't hear the message. You can tell me you have heard this message and then turn around and do the same thing that got you into trouble. This is the disease. If the disease is not treated, that's the way it works. You can think you're loaded with good information and turn around and stumble, quick as hell. I can go back forty-four years and pick up my old thinking, just like that, because of this disease. What brought me here is still here. Believe me, I know this.

But you can have a spiritual awakening. I know this, too. I've had more than one, and I know I'll keep having them because what we're talking about here is the grace of God. What we have here is an undeserved gift. On page 125 of the Twelve by Twelve, it says:

> These little studies of A.A.'s Twelve Steps now come to a close. We have been considering so many problems that it may appear that A.A. consists mainly of racking dilemmas and troubleshooting. To a certain extent, that is true. We have been talking about problems because we are problem people who have found a way up and out, and who wish to share our knowledge of this way with all who can use it. For it is only by accepting and solving our problems that we can begin to get right with ourselves and with the world about us, and with Him who presides over us all. Understanding is the key to right principles and attitudes and right action is the key to good living. Therefore the joy of good living is the theme of A.A. Twelve Steps.

It says we are a "problem people." Now I don't know about you, but I was always wrapped up in my problems. I didn't always know it, though. When I got into this program, I got into building a new character and looking at the world a little differently. But I'd still turn back to my problems because I still had the same attitude. Now these problems were an obstacle to my relationship, with God, and with the program. I always figured that if I could just get rid of my problems, I would be okay. But did you ever stop to think about what happens when you get rid of a problem? Here comes another problem. And then another, right behind it. That's the disease of alcoholism. That was a pretty tough nut for me to swallow. I thought I was pretty smart because I had a job, I was making money, I was clean-shaven, and I wasn't falling down drunk anymore. You'd have thought that was supposed to give me an edge or something and that I wouldn't go on and do the same dumb thing I had always done. But these things didn't help a bit. My head was still wacky. And this head of mine is the authority for my life. It'll keep doing the same thing it's always done.

But if you apply these Steps, you build a new character. When you get to Step Twelve, you've had a spiritual awakening as a result of all the Steps that went before. Now you've got a character that is not self-conscious. It's God-conscious. Now you're backed up by spiritual principles, with a brain that's not ratty, selfish, and self-centered. You're not full of defects of character. This brain is occupied by a power greater than yourself, meaning God. This is what this program of recovery is all about. This is not something we can figure out on our own. It only happens by the grace of God. This is the guarantee for each one of us. With these Steps, we can live in the world and be happy. We can do things that we could never do before. My heavenly Father is going to give me what I need all along the way, right up to this very minute. When I acknowledge God's presence in my life, I can live every moment, right now. And I can thank God for my yesteryears and praise him for them.

This message is about a way of life, as far as I'm concerned. It's about a way of life that each and every one of us can have. We don't have to live in a ratty world, full of hurts and harms. I don't have to live in a world that I take from all the time and am still never satisfied. I can give back. I can make this world a better place. I can count my blessings. I can name my blessings. I don't just say, "Thanks, God." I thank him for each and every day, for everything that's in the day. I name people. I name things. I acknowledge to God his presence in my life. This is what I need to do in my life.

▲ Can you say more about what is meant by a "spiritual awakening"?

A spiritual awakening, for me, is anything out of the ordinary, or anything that's hooked up to a power greater than me. A spiritual awakening is recognizing there is a power that's called God. That alone is a spiritual awakening. In my book it is. "Having had a spiritual awakening as a result of these steps" means that I have applied the other eleven Steps. In the course of applying these Steps, I have been able to identify and see and recognize the need of a power greater than me which is called God. This God is a power in my life and in all my affairs. So a spiritual awakening is a way of life that is continuous. It isn't a blinding flash. It doesn't happen all at once. My spiritual awakening happened piecemeal.

I learned by trial and error. For example, a piece came to me in Step Three. I started to do something in Step Three. I started to trust another man, an alcoholic. I started to listen to him. I started to pray to his God. And it started becoming very self-evident to me that I was doing something to change me. I was getting rid of a dirty, rotten world, and I was starting to see a world that wasn't so dirty and rotten. It was becoming evident to me that if I could grow with what little I was doing, why couldn't I go for more? And I did go for more. So I try something else and maybe it benefits me. And I try another thing and it works. It's a continuous thing, it's an everyday thing, it's an all day thing, it's a forever thing. But it happens in only one day, and that's the day I'm in.

Summing Up

Questions & Answers

In previous chapters, I noted that I keep saying the same things over and over again. The reason I do this is that I need to hear these things over and over again. Whether you hear them in the same way, I don't know. But this is the character that I am today.

A long time ago, I started to find a different way of life. I found this program. But having found it, I couldn't stop. I had to keep this character building going. I can't look backwards and congratulate myself because I'm better than I used to be and so now I can do as I please. No, I can't do as I please. I still have to apply the Steps today. I still have to apply each Step so that I can become a new character. The new character that I am today has to progress daily by applying the principles found in the Steps, not just by applying the Steps. You see, it changes in the Twelfth Step. Before the Twelfth Step, you have to apply the Steps themselves. But the Twelfth Step says that we have to "apply these principles in all our affairs." That's a heck of a statement right there, but I couldn't get it because somebody was always saying "you didn't do Step Four well enough" and things like that. That may be good advice and it may apply to you. Maybe you didn't do Step Four well enough, but it doesn't cut it to say that you only need something special in your Step application and your troubles will go away. I know it doesn't cut it because the moment you lose touch with this program of recovery or with God, there are no Steps to be practiced.

Why should you keep coming to this program? Why would you keep coming here, day after day, week after week, and year after year? Do you keep coming because you missed a certain application of a certain Step? To be a new character, you have to be this new character *now*. You have to grow spiritually *now*. You have to use the principles found in this program *now*. You can't get to some point in the steps and stop. You have to go forward. Maybe you're afraid. Maybe you're lost. But you go forward. Total dependency on a power greater than myself, on God, is the strength and power I have to rely on day in and day out. I can only do that through character building. I can only build character through the process found in the Steps.

This is why you should look at Step Two all the time. Are you talking to God or to yourself? Do you believe in yourself so much that you would go there instead of to God? These are questions that help me in my thinking and doing. How do I stay away from me? I can't even stay away from me by myself. It's impossible. I need the strength of a higher power.

The message of this program is found in the Twelve Steps, not in meetings and readings. They're important, but you can't build this new character just by reading or listening at meetings. You can attend all the meetings you want and still remain the same character. I know that. I did it. You can't build the new character just by staying sober. I know that. I was sober and my character didn't change. Your character does not change just by knowing the Steps. I was taught the Steps from the word "go," but I didn't know them in application. I didn't know the message that you can find in the Twelve Steps. You have to make this program a way of life.

If you do, you can build a new character and live in a new world. Now it blows me away that every one of us—it doesn't matter what gender you are, what color you are, or what country you're from—can have a continuous, growing, good life. You can have relationships with people that you never had before. Page 53 of the Twelve by Twelve tells me that I have failed to recognize my "total inability to form a true partnership with another human being." That's what I'm talking about. This program of recovery makes it possible to build a new character that doesn't have to live in that world. Why not live in a good world? Why not have a world that's waiting for you? Why listen to something and keep stumbling and struggling? Why listen to somebody else who says, "You can't do this or you shouldn't do that"? You don't need to live that way. I know this, and I'm no guru. I'm a messenger. When I live this message, as it is in print, I can have exactly what it says I'll have.

Here are some concluding questions that I've been asked.

▲ One of the things I've heard you talk about in the past is the book *The Sermon on the Mount*, by Emmett Fox. How can you go deeper into the Twelve Steps by reading this book?

A long time ago, in the early 1950s, I had a sponsor who tried to pound the Steps into me, but I just couldn't hear the things that I needed to do to apply the Steps. Then I heard this gal named Inez M. talk about *The Sermon on the Mount* and how it helped her find a power that was helping her in her life. I liked the way she talked and I figured if she could do it, I could do it. So I went out and bought a copy of *The Sermon on the Mount*. The Beatitudes, as Emmett Fox described them, told me how to do some things that were required by the Steps but that I couldn't seem to get from the Steps themselves. So I started to use whatever I could find in The Sermon on the Mount to help me apply the Steps, not to apply *The Sermon on the Mount*. This book didn't replace the

Twelve Steps. It did not. But it helped me to see things that I couldn't get directly from the Steps and in that way it helped me apply the Steps themselves. *The Sermon on the Mount* told me exactly what to do. And that's what I needed to apply the Steps. Now maybe you can read the Steps and know exactly what to do. Or maybe somebody could tell you what to do. But I just got lost all the time. I'd go out in the world and all of sudden I'm with myself again and I can't do nothing different than I did before. I mean well, but I can't do well.

When I work with alkies, I never introduce *The Sermon on the Mount* until I'm sure they have something in their lives they can call a power greater than themselves. And there's no way I'm going to tell any of you to go outside the program to read anything. If you tell me, as a baby of mine, that you're doing stuff outside of the program, but you're out there throwing fits and punishing your wife, I'm going to tell you to get back into this program of recovery. You better leave that outside stuff alone. You better find out what this program is all about or you're going to wind up drunk or insane, or you'll kill yourself. I don't preach to anybody, but you better realize, as I have, that the message is the Twelve Steps.

There is a language that we use in this program. For a long time, I didn't know this language. I didn't know that, as I walk in the day I'm in, this language keeps me alive. Words like "willingness" and "Step application." Now Step application is not the application of the Steps, it's the application of principles. You learn the Steps by the numbers. This keeps you where you belong. You learn by the numbers so you can put the Steps in a logical order and build character by going from Step One to Step Twelve, not from Step Twelve to Step One or whatever way you wish to do it. Now I don't know if you think this is stupid, but I did at one time. If you told me to, I would do the Steps in order, from One to Twelve. But then I'd forget who I was and I might try to jump from Step One to Step Ten. I used to do that all the time. You know how I did it? Step One is where I'd admit I was an alcoholic and Step Ten is where I was sorry about it. I'd go around telling everyone, "I'm an alcoholic, I'm sorry." So I only did Step One and Step Ten all the time.

This is important. Maybe you have the trouble I had. Maybe you do things that are not too cool. Maybe you get into trouble. Maybe you turn. Maybe you don't treat everybody the same way. Why not find out about this? Why not at least be presented with it? Keep an open mind. That's why Step Two comes so early—so that your mind doesn't slam shut. You don't need to quarrel with this because you don't need to do this program of recovery if you don't want to. But at least let these ideas be presented. Maybe you might need part of what I'm saying, maybe none of it, maybe all of it. Who knows? But don't close your mind off to it. "Willingness" is a principle that allows me to walk and talk, today, with an open mind. When I walk and talk today, I am surrendered. I have surrendered my old self. I did not end my old self or quit doing something. I surrendered. I stopped doing me and I started doing the program of recovery with God. And so I built a new character. Surrendering is both an ending and a beginning. That's a true surrender.

I had to face this. If I surrendered, what would I do? What would I have? I had to have something. So I read *The Sermon on the Mount*. I have done this every day for twenty-eight years. I read a page, two pages, maybe I read a chapter, maybe I read the whole Beatitudes. I found out that if I started my morning by doing this reading, I would be able to go farther into the day before I lost it. At that time, I recognized that this growth was because I took a little time, I slowed down, I read something that took myself away from me. If I stayed away from me long enough, I could add a little something to my life. That's the purpose of Step Two—to give you an open mind. To make you receptive to something other than yourself.

▲ You have said a lot about building a relationship with a living God. Can you say something more about that?

When I came here, I didn't have anything going for me in the way of churches, prayer, religious background or God. I had no information. Now I don't believe that having a belief or a religious background qualifies me for spiritual success. If I had some religious background, the odds of my success would not have been any better. Whatever I brought into this program, I have to give up in order to build a new character. Whether I had a God or didn't, whether I went to church or didn't, whatever I had that brought me here, I have to give that up. On page 58 of the Big Book, it says, "Some of us have tried to hold onto our old ideas and the result was nil until we let go absolutely." What are my old ideas? Whatever my mind can produce. Whatever comes out of my mind. I have to start realizing what the Steps are for. When Step Two says that I came to believe in a power greater than myself that could restore me to sanity, what was that? How can I have something like this before I have even turned my life and my will over to the care of a power greater than myself, whatever that is? In Step One, when it said my life was unmanageable, I found out my life was unmanageable drunk or sober, rich or poor. It makes no difference. But what am I, if I stay with myself and my life's unmanageable? I'm an alcoholic with alcoholism. Now in the front half of Step One, they talk about alcohol. But in the second part, they are talking about alcoholism. Who I am, what I am, and why I do what I do is already established. My life is all about me. But Step Two says that I'm going to have to do something different now, and the only way that I can do that is by having an open mind. If I can keep my mind from slamming shut, I've got a chance. If I go to a power greater than myself—instead of to the power of self—then I've got a chance. Notice that this Step doesn't refer to God. It doesn't even say "Higher Power." It just says a power that is greater than myself. Now this makes it acceptable. You can't wiggle out of it. You can't tell me that you can't have the Steps in your life. All the Steps are written in this way. When Bill W. was writing these Steps, he kept reviewing them, reviewing them, reviewing them. They had to find a way to put the thing into words that you couldn't wiggle out of. And everything in these Steps was written in the past tense. "Here are the Steps we took," as it says on page 59 of the Big Book. They took them. They didn't read about them. They didn't talk about them. They took them. They applied them. So Step Two is where I came to believe in a power that's greater than me. Because it doesn't name that power, I'm at least willing to look at what they mean. If they had said, "I have to come to believe in God," I wouldn't have done it. I would have walked away and I might have killed myself over it. I don't know. And by Step Three I'm ready to name this power as "God" but only with the qualification "as I understood him." Now this was something I never understood. I always thought you had to believe in somebody's God—your God, my father's God, whoever. I never wanted none of that. I don't want your stuff. I don't want to believe like you. I don't even like you. I'm programmed to argue. I'm programmed to tell you that whatever you believe is bullcrap. That's me. To get away from me, I have to open my mind up. That's the requirement now. How can I build a relationship with anything other than myself when I'm preoccupied with myself all the time? So why don't I try to build a relationship with this power greater than myself? Why not talk to something other than myself and get some results now? Now at this point, I have an open mind. I have the willingness to try something else instead of saying "baloney." So I learned how to talk to something other than myself. I did it the same way I used to train my dogs. You talk to the dog. You keep his attention. You share everything with him about the traffic, about the weather, about this and that. You talk to him and his ears stick up. He's alert. He hears you. So I learned to talk to something other than me, and I knew that I wasn't talking to myself because I wasn't telling myself what to do all the time. This is where I learned about self-talking as a form of power. Self-talking is the power of self. Don't get this mixed up with thinking. It's not. Self-talking is where I tell myself that you're wrong. Self-talking is where I tell myself everything should be different from what it is. I don't know how much self-talking you do, but I used to do it all day long.

I'm not telling you to get on your hands and knees to build your relationship with God. But you have to talk to something other than yourself. I had to, and I learned how to do it. Now I can do it all morning long. I do it by thanking him, praising him. I acknowledge his presence. I don't pray to him in the sense that I am putting a petition out there or something like that. I'm discussing my life with him. I'm telling God that I'm very happy because he's in my life. This is a relationship with a power that's greater than me. I can always have a better thought in my head by talking to God instead of to myself. Every time I talk to myself, I get into trouble. My opinion might be good or bad. It don't make no difference. I still have an opinion and this opinion is what influences my life. This kind of self-talking is what messes up my life. So why not have something there besides myself?

Whatever you want to name it or however you want to do it, I don't care. At least make the effort. At least try to develop this relationship and see what you get out of it. I'll tell you what, if you have a relationship with a higher power, it will stop you in your tracks when you get mean and mad. When you're storming inside and you're looking at someone with ferocious eyes, this relationship will stop you cold. Try it and see what happens to your eyes and your thinking. The thinking will go—darn near instantly. It just leaves. So now you're doing something different than you did before. You're under another power. You're allowing something else to be there. You're letting go. You're stopping one thing and beginning another. You're building a relationship.

To build a relationship right now, why can't any one of us talk to God? Why can't we praise him and thank him for allowing us to be alive, to read a book, or to have whatever we need in the moment we're in? Why not acknowledge the good things in your life? Praise God and thank him for those things. Keep his presence in your mind.

This is how I live. This is what I do. All the time. I'm not saying I do this to perfection. But I do the best I can do in the day I'm in and I let God be there for me.

▲ I tend to complicate things. Now I've got a lot of new information. How do I keep it simple?

The new character is how you do it. It's as simple as that. You have to build a new character by applying the Twelve Steps. If you do the Twelve Steps, it isn't a question of being the old character anymore. You're a new character in the day you're in, wherever you are in the Steps. They are in a logical order. When you are applying the Steps, in order, you are getting what you need to build a new character in the day you're in. You do Step One, and then Step Two, and then Step Three and so on down the line.

Often people ask me if you can go back to a previous Step and pick up something you missed. You can do it. Certainly, you can do it. But you can also change as you're building the new character. This is an application. This is a building thing. If I'm talking to one of my babies and I find out he's having trouble, I don't assume he did something wrong. I assume I did something wrong. So I take him back to the ABCs, and then Step One, and Step Two, and Step Three. I want to help him identify just what he has inside him as a new character. When he can see this, then and only then he can go farther ahead.

You have to make the right kind of beginning. The application of these Steps has to be there for your character to change.

How can I go ahead to Step Four if I know Step Three but not Step One or Step Two? It's impossible. I can't do it. I left out the application of Steps One and Two. I'm in deep trouble. I don't admit that I'm powerless over alcohol. I don't even know what that means, so somewhere down the line I'm going to think alcohol is needed. I didn't start building my relationship with a power greater than me because I didn't do Step Two. I'm in deep trouble again because I'm just going to listen to myself all over again.

So you have to get into the application of these Steps. Just as the slogan says, first things first. Apply these Steps in order and you will have what you need. It's that simple. This message is meant for all alcoholics. And it works. Once this message is delivered, you won't have to blow your brains out. I really believe that. I've seen this in the lives of different alkies and in mine, too. Without this message, I'm lost. I'm dead. I'm living in a world that keeps turning upside down all the time. This message has to be delivered. It's not my message. I don't have a message. Everything I've said is in the literature.

▲ I have heard you talk about the two-fold nature of alcoholism, about the physical allergy and the mental obsession. I always equated the mental obsession with the obsession to drink, but what I've heard you say is that the mental obsession is the alcoholic insanity, or stinking thinking, that makes the world upside down all the time. Could you elaborate on this?

The mental obsession is described in the beginning of Step One. The mental obsession is about more than an urge to drink. Chapter 3 of the Big Book talks about how the disease affects my thinking processes and makes me think I can drink just like my non-alcoholic fellows. I become an obsessed character. But my obsession is not just about drinking. As an alcoholic, I have become someone who doesn't know how to have a little bit of this or a little bit of that. I'm obsessed with everything. My obsession may have started out with alcohol, but it's the obsession that is important. It is a mental condition, a condition of the mind.

Now the physical allergy component to the disease, as opposed to the mental obsession, is something I can treat one hundred percent. That's because I can stop putting alcohol into me and the allergy won't manifest itself. Now this allergy isn't breaking out in hives. It's breaking out in jails, in institutions, in losing jobs, and losing spouses and all that. What is a physical allergy? It's not like somebody eating strawberries and breaking out in hives. Now if you stop eating strawberries, your hives go away and they don't come back. That's not what this allergy is like. This allergy is the purpose that I have in all my affairs. My life gets ratty. It gets rotten. It turns on the world. This is not my mind turning on the world—it's my body. This is a physical allergy. I had to look at how this worked for me. One time when I was drunk I hit a barricade of police cruisers head on. I never even saw them. That's the allergy at work, not the mental obsession. With a physical allergy, my body doesn't function right.

Now my mental obsession became a way of life. I'd say to myself, "I'm not going to drink. I'm going to go straight home from work. I'm going to get all cleaned up, then I'm going to take her out to dinner." But my mental obsession would say, "No, you're not going to do that at all. You're going to go down to the bar and suck on that juice because that's where your life is. That's where your happiness is." My mental obsession hooked me up to a life where everything revolved around drinking. The drinking, for me, was the world I wanted to be in. This was a good world, but it was killing me and I didn't even know it.

Now today, ever since I got out of the hospital, I haven't had the mental obsession to drink. Never once. I don't know if that's because of the hospital experience or because I hit bottom hard enough to knock some sense into me. But I don't fight the mental obsession anymore. I just don't think it's a good idea to go and smother my world with alcohol any more. I don't know if this is a struggle for you or if you still wonder if you're an alcoholic. I get a lot of babies like that. They don't want to be alcoholics. In fact, they're angry about it. "Why the heck do I have to be an alcoholic? Why can't I go out and act like other people?" I got one like that just recently. That's a mental obsession, not an allergy. The mental obsession is talking to them, telling them something. As soon as their day doesn't turn out too smoothly, they go into denial. "Why in the hell do I have to be an alcoholic? Why can't I be like everybody else and go out there and have a little fun? Why can't I have a drink?" Now I never did have that kind of fun and today I don't have an obsession to drink. I don't know about you.

▲ This is another "how do you do it?" question. I have heard you talk about building a relationship with God and how that's something you don't do all in one stroke. I have heard you talk about talking to that power when you're angry. Being angry is something I struggle with on an almost daily basis. A few months back, my spiritual state was as good or better than it had ever been. I had gotten up and done some reading and some writing that morning. When I talked to people during the day, I commented on how good I felt. Well, in the afternoon, someone that I do a lot of business with did something that could have gotten the company into hot water with the IRS. I lost it immediately and couldn't get my sanity back. I wasn't unconscious about it. I was even aware of how ironic it was that I had been in such a good space in the morning and was now practicing my old character with a vengeance. Do you have any suggestions as to what a person might do?

When I talk about building a new character, I'm talking about living as a new character today. I'm not talking about living with the old character until I complete the Steps. The old character is me, my mind, as the power. When I have a power greater than myself and a method, I am able to stay in the new character. My mind doesn't have to search out and go where it wants to go because of anger. The old character is there, but it isn't there to act on because there is a power greater than myself that is walking with me. The idea that you can walk and talk with a power greater than yourself in all your affairs is hard to get.

When we talk about "all your affairs," we're talking about how you live your life in all of its details. This is hard because when you get down to your real life, as you're living it each day, you're going to want to keep going back to your old self and that's where the anger lies. It doesn't lie in your new character. Now when you go through Steps Four, Five, and Six, you reach a point where you're ready to have God remove all your defects of character. This is a lifetime job. No matter who you are as an alcoholic, you don't have to live life like you used to anymore. You do not have to live in pain and suffering all the time because your mind is thinking something. You have a God-consciousness. You have lost your self-consciousness. Because of my God-consciousness, I don't have to respond to things in my life with all my defects of character. I don't have to come at life with my self or with my memory. This new character business is a hard concept to get across. I keep pounding, pounding, pounding, saying the same thing all over again, hoping you'll hear it.

When you look at things from an alcoholic point of view, you think in terms of things you should be doing or shouldn't be doing. But why not get to the point where you don't have to look for trouble or even worry about identifying trouble? There is a way to live without all the pain and suffering, the hurts, the harm, and all the bad stuff that goes on in your life. There is a way to do this. That why this is called a program of recovery.

This program of recovery was started on June 10, 1935, by Dr. Bob, Bill Wilson, and God so that each and every one of us could have something we never had before—a method of living based on a higher power. Now it's not easy to change your focus from your self to a higher power. When you get a thought you energize it, it becomes real, you entertain it, and you can't change it because you lack the power. That's what it means on page 45 of the Big Book. Lack of power is your dilemma. But you can do something—if you're willing to go to any lengths to have what we have and if you're willing to take the Twelve Steps.

▲ I have trouble with my mind. Now I don't have to wake up and think, "Oh, my God, it's doomsday," or anything like that. But maybe the neighbor kids get on my nerves. Or maybe a couple of people I work with don't perform the way I think they should perform. So maybe I'll find myself ridiculing these people behind their backs. Now God may present to me that these are pretty nice human beings, but part of me just doesn't want to stop bad-mouthing them. In my heart, I know this is wrong because my father always told me to help people instead of talking about them. But I do it anyway. That's where I get stuck. Does this make sense?

Yes, sure it makes sense. Emmett Fox, in his *The Sermon on the Mount*, refers to thoughts as enemy soldiers that dig in and can't be dug out easily. This is what you're talking about. What upsets me, I had to learn, is not what people are doing but what my mind tells me they are doing. Now that's a son of a gun. My brain tells me they're doing something bad, whether they're doing something bad or not. That's what my brain is telling me. That's what Dr. Silkworth is referring to when he says that alcoholics drink for the effect because their minds are restless, irritable, and discontent. That's alcoholism, not drunkenness. There is something wrong with our minds—your mind, my mind. We have to look at this because we just can't get everybody to do what we want them to do. That's the definition of an unmanageable life—constantly trying to get people to do what you want them to do. To accept another person, whether it be your spouse, your neighbor, a co-worker, or whoever, is a difficult thing to accomplish if you're not treating your alcoholism. But you can do it. There is a way. That's what this program of recovery is all about. I can have something in my life that I've never had before, a power greater than myself. A power that can do for me what I can't do for myself.

Now I know I'm repeating myself, but I have to do this. The average person has to hear something sixteen times before they can take it in. Now if it takes the average person sixteen times to actually hear something, it must take me 116 times. That's because of the power of self. That because I have a mind that is injured, that is hurt, that is denying things.

▲ I do a decent job of applying these principles in my personal and private life. Where I come into conflict is in my business life. I hire people. Unfortunately, when you hire people, you have to fire people. When I evaluate someone, I find it difficult to determine whether to let them go or to go another step in trying to facilitate a change in their working life so that they can keep their job. The same thing happens when I'm working with someone in the program. I can't tell when I'm doing more harm than good and should let go of them or whether there is something I should change to help the relationship to continue. When I try to find God's will, I only find my own. How do I apply the principles in these affairs?

Building your character is a lifetime job. It isn't something you can do at certain places, at certain times. You have to build this new character wherever you are. You have to take God into your work as a boss. You have to take God into your bedroom. Your character isn't built for some things and not for others.

I have to be the character that God wants me to be. I can hire people and I can fire people. I have hired people. And I've had to fire them because they were incompetent. You have the right to run your business the way it should be run. You have the intelligence God wants you to have. If this program is a way of life, you have to be able to look at the world in a way that allows you to let somebody go without wanting to hurt them. The point is, you have to practice these principles in all your affairs. You don't have to drink or die or go insane. My mind doesn't do what it used to do. It doesn't abuse people, hurt people, take advantage of them, or throw them away. If I build this new character, I should be able to walk through the world and face whatever it presents.

You've always got your own will. You can throw all this out whenever you want to. The difference for me today is that you can no longer take these principles away from me. You can't make me go out into the world and want to rip somebody apart. You can't make me want to hurt you at all. Before coming to this program, someone could upset me so bad I couldn't even eat. You can't do that to me now. The reason is that there is a power in my life that's greater than me, that says there is no way I'm going to respond like that.

You can't take it from me, but I can throw it away. I can walk away from this program of recovery. I can walk away from God. I can walk away from the Twelve Steps and do my own thing. This is the free will that God gave me.

▲ This is another question about managing people. I don't want to manage people the way I used to. I was dictatorial. I was always right. Even when I'm right, I have to be really right. Now I want that new character you're talking about. I'm trying to envision how to develop this character, but I can't really do it. I just don't want to boss people around anymore. I want them to be involved in a happy family and to be happy with what they're doing. Now I know that if I hire people, sometimes I'm going to have to fire them. But I'd like to have happy employees because they make for happy customers.

Now you're bringing up the ego factor. I think I'm

somebody special because I'm the boss or the owner of the business. I'm in a different category, and I get to look down on people. I can dictate their lives. If they don't do things my way, I can fire them.

When I got violently mad, I thought this was just alcoholism. But it's not just that. There's a character inside me full of ego. That's the self. Most of this ego thing is in the unconscious mind. So in order to do something about this ego, you have to bring it to the surface and talk about it. Otherwise, in the day I'm in, the ego will overpower me and become the power. When you work the Steps, this ego problem is being treated, especially when you get to Step Seven. In Step Seven, you learn to give instead of take. And in Step Ten, when you take a personal inventory and promptly admit when you're wrong, you stop the ego right there. When you live by these Steps, your ego will get smaller, the new character will get stronger, and you will get closer to God.

As alcoholics, you and I have certain ways of looking at life so that we can handle it. We do things under protest or under half-steam. Maybe we're forced into doing something we don't want to do. Then we're upset and doing something under protest. This is our ego at work, controlling us.

Maybe you see it in your workers. They're slam-banging things around, cussing and swearing. That's the way I was all the time. I was dangerous because I was doing something that I had to but I hated every minute of it. I was complying instead of surrendering. I couldn't surrender my life of fighting and arguing. I couldn't become happy, joyous, and free. My ego kept me over in the crap all the time. I was macho. I thought I was so smart and so right, that I knew more than you.

Whether you're an employer or an employee don't make no difference. This is the same. You can do what you have to do. Like you said, some of your employees will come and some will have to go. But you don't have to get all upset about it.

You don't have to punish people. You don't have to be so iron-fisted that everyone is uncomfortable.

▲ You gave some examples about how you talk to this God in your life. Could you be more precise about this?

In the beginning, I didn't know how to pray. I had to be taught. So I was taught to call my higher power "God," to get on my knees, to do this in the morning and the evening and whenever I could during the day. It was a beginning, and any kind of beginning is good. Nobody can tell you how to pray. But they can identify some things that you do now and that you can do in the future. For example, I didn't know I could pray at work. I learned I didn't need to get on my knees or go into the bathroom or anything like that. I could just talk to God, right now, this minute, right there at work. I could have this relationship with God. I didn't need to get on my knees or make it into a ritual. I can do that, but I don't need to in order to have a relationship with God.

This is a living God. This is something that I had to learn because I was used to keeping God out of my life. I felt that God was needed only in certain places and certain times. In Step Eleven, I learned that I could improve my conscious contact with God and that I could have a relationship with God right now. Whether I have trouble at the moment or not doesn't make no difference to a living God. Today I walk and talk with a power greater than myself. When I did Step Three, I turned my will and my life over to the care of God. Now I get a daily reprieve, like the Big Book says. Every day that I carry the vision of God's will instead of my own into my activities, I get that daily reprieve.

I could have this God with me in all my affairs. Whether I'm an employer or an employee doesn't make any difference. I can be whatever God wants me to be in the day I'm in. I can be a good boss with a few mechanics working for me. I can have a good relationship with my wife. I don't keep God out of my life, thinking that he belongs in some areas and not in others. This is a living God.

This was hard for me to understand. I was so programmed to think that I had to get on my knees and petition God for something at a certain time and place—when I was in trouble. I didn't know how to meditate. To me, it didn't make any sense. They wanted me to meditate in the morning when I first woke up. Why? I figured I should meditate during the day when things were going wrong, when I was in court and they were taking all my stuff, when I was on the operating table. I didn't know that meditating was quietness, listening, receiving something in my mind instead of sending out a message.

I got one baby who goes into surgery with me all the time. I go in there—now I've been in there about sixty times—and he's standing beside me and he tells me later that when they're putting me out, I'm still talking to God. Imagine that! I'm able to keep this conscious contact alive in those conditions. This is what it is all about. This relationship with God is what makes a program of recovery. It's not the relationship with myself. I have that naturally. God don't dress me, brush my teeth, or anything else. But I need something more than me in my life. I need something in my mind, something that enables me to live in the world because it's a good world.

▲ There was something wrong with my world. Why? Because I was in the picture. Because I said to myself that I knew the answers. If only I could solve this little problem, everything would be dandy. I'd have happy employees. I'd do the right thing. Nothing could change in my life until I got to the point where I'd go to God no matter what was going on and accept whatever God gave me. Even today, I catch myself. God will correct me and say, "Hey, you're doing it again." You're assuming something is in place, and it's not. What's not in place is that dependency and trust and reliance on a higher power, no matter what's bugging me. When I'm confused, it's not the confusion out there that's bugging me. It's the confusion between my ears that's really the problem.

Yeah, you're talking about the need to keep looking inwardly, all the time. You can't be looking outwardly. What I'm talking about is looking at the world and always finding fault with everything outside of yourself. I've got an overactive brain that is full of me and all kinds of judgment about everybody else. I have to be looking inwardly, at myself and not at somebody else. And I can't be caught up in the past or in the future. I have to be looking at myself now. This program of recovery has to be about now. If it's not about now, it's going to be about never. I say this all the time because it took me so long to hear it, and I need to hear it over and over again to this day. If it isn't now, it'll never happen.

▲ Did you, early in your recovery, use any gimmicks to keep yourself on track?

Sure, I'd use whatever I could to get me back to where I belong. One thing I learned about was ominous signs. The minute I showed judgment, criticism, worry, anger, resentment, I knew I was losing it. When I'm intolerant of who you are, I'm getting off track. This is the disease.

Here's an example. I go to Costco all the time and I get impatient with their long lines at the checkout. Whether you go early in the morning or late at night, it seems like they're long. Everybody's got a basketful. So I see another line with a person with only three items in his basket and I hot-foot it over there. Now I'm in the good line, but I look over to where I used to be and that line is starting to move. Now my line is stuck because this guy with only three items is trying to write a check but he can't seem to get it done. I'm wondering what the heck is going on here. Another guy comes along and wants to cut through our line to get to that other line. So I let him pass me. Next thing I see is him checking out, and I'm still standing there. I'm still in the same place. I go crazy over stuff like that. I'll take it out on the store. I'll take it out on the road. I'll take it out on you. This could still happen to me today, which is why this disease has to be treated now, on this day. These may not seem like big things, but this is where the disease operates and this is how the disease can ruin your day. This is why this can't be a program of recovery for yesterday. It has to be a program of recovery for the day you're in.

▲ I was talking to someone yesterday, and I had the thought that it's not as good today as it was yesterday. I get an overwhelmed feeling when I'm angry. I know this has to do with self and the disease of alcoholism, but this is a frightening place to be. All of a sudden, I'm blind as a bat and I don't know what's going on. Where do I go from here?

You know, there is no reason to think of yesterday, but I'll think about it. And those thoughts will affect me too. So I had to learn that this program of recovery is about the application of the Twelve Steps. Never can I get away from that. It's like a closed circuit. My whole life is wrapped up in the Twelve Steps. My whole life. Everything is there, and I don't need to go outside of those Steps. The only time this is a program of recovery is when I am doing those Twelve Steps. This was a hard thing to get across to the old me because I always wanted to take over. I'm the power. I think I'm entitled. Or I think I have the right to say what I want and do what I want. I think I shouldn't be bothered with things I don't want to do. I shouldn't be bothered with having to cut the grass or go to the market. Wherever my mind goes, the disease is still there. The whole package of self. There isn't one thought that causes me trouble. It's my whole mind. That's why I have to put this program of recovery into all my affairs.

▲ Can you say something about "safe ground"?

"Safe ground" is something I learned about piecemeal. I learned about it in small degrees. Each time I got past something, each time I learned something, each time I got results that were pretty good, I got onto safe ground. I start to think that from here on out, things are going to be perfect. It gives me the false impression that I don't have to apply the Steps, do the reading, do the praying, or do any of those things. All of a sudden I'm talking to myself again. I had to learn to get the heck away from that kind of thinking. There is no safe ground for me. All I've got is a daily reprieve. This is a now thing. This program of recovery is something that I must have all of the time, right now, even here.

▲ I was introduced to the concept of writing on a daily basis when I first came into the program. I was told it was an important outlet. I'm curious about your opinion of this as a tool.

I do a lot of writing. I've done this over the years. But I don't do it like an inventory. It's more a displaying of my mind, what it's doing and what it knows. Some of my babies write every day, and I go through it every day with them. This is good, but I'm not telling you that you have to do this.

Don't hear this wrong. Sometimes I write a lot. Sometimes I don't. It's like reading. I read a lot. I read for three, four, five hours at a time. But I'm not telling you to do this. It's just that my life is important to me, and what I do is what I have to do. You don't have to read as much as I do. But you must read daily from the literature if you want to grow and you want to learn about the vocabulary that we've been talking about. Otherwise you are going to be caught up in newspapers and television or wherever your mind has been. Now when I write, I date everything. I might write a lot. I might write a little. On August 18, 1994, the only thing I wrote was, "Will power pledges mutual aid. Fixed truths. Personality changes. Spiritual conversions. Unity on vital essentials. Willed not by the individual. Surrender: an unconscious event." Now this is information. Usually I get what I write from the Big Book, Dr. Tiebout's papers, the Twelve by Twelve, or something like that. This is up to the individual. But it's not an inventory. I'm not looking for that. What I read today might say something to me, and writing it down will help me look at it. This helps keep your mind active and looking to do more.

▲ Could you elaborate on what you meant when you said your life was important to you?

The main thing is that I have had to define what life is. I learned that "life" is not the same as "living." My life is internal. My life is the character I represent. My life isn't "out there" at all. It's in here. I had to learn this by trial and error. For a long time, I thought that my life was making money, being with women, being a boss, or being smarter than you. Stuff like that. In other words, it took material satisfactions to please me. I was always struggling to achieve more or to get more. This was the wrong direction. I wasn't treating my mind. I was still the same character. I was staying sober, and I thought that was the name of the game. I was obsessed with winning, but my "life" was never really important to me.

That's what Step Seven is all about. Step Seven tells you that spiritual values and character building have to come first. Material satisfactions are not the final end and aim of life. Now if I say my life is important to me, I mean that I care about my mind and how I think. I care about my character. You can't get this from reading. You can't get it from meetings. Nobody talks about it. You have to figure this out for yourself. You have to learn the difference between living and life. The love that you show to your family—that's life. That's where your success is. That's where your happiness is. The Steps lead you to this. Step Seven, especially, is important. When the literature talks about "serving and God," it's talking about life, not living. It's talking about performing in the day you're in—not to make money, not to get bigger cars, not to get more women. This is about your mind. This is about your character.

▲ Could you give a definition of the word "principles"? What are some of the principles?

I had to change this word to "truths." When I was out in the world, I had too many variables in my life. I couldn't get connected to principles. One minute I was okay; one minute I was in trouble. One minute I was happy; the next minute I was sad. One minute I wanted to help you; the next minute I won't help you. One minute I'm building a new character; the next minute I'm full of my old, selfish self. When they talked about principles, I couldn't connect. So I changed the word to "truth," but it's the same thing really because a truth has to come from a principle. The principles are spiritual in nature, and they had to become a way of life for me or I wouldn't have benefited from them. Now the only way I can benefit from them is by applying them to my life, not by reading about them or talking about them. In Step Two, I started to learn to build a new character away from the old character. When I started here, I was angry and hostile. I was suspicious, jealous, envious. I was a liar. I was a person who would take advantage of everything and anything for no apparent reason. I had been building my life, but not on spiritual principles. I built it on what I thought I needed and wanted. That's why I had to do the Fourth Step, the Fifth Step, and the Sixth Step. When they talk about principles, they are talking about how to identify my defects of character, how to admit them to God and to myself and another human being, and how to become ready to have God remove them. To have my alcoholism treated, I have to be reborn. I have to become a new character. There's nothing that I brought here that I can use. I have to start new and I have to start with the principles laid down in the literature.

I don't know what you need in your life, but the first thing I needed was to learn how to live without anger. I had to live without a hostile mind. How can I do that without a principle? When we were talking about Step One, we talked about the principle found in that Step; namely, that I cannot ever take alcohol into my body again. Ever. Now there's a principle. Now that's a principle I can do one hundred percent. I do not have to drink. And so long as I don't drink, my allergy will be treated. But what about my mental obsession? What am I going to do about that? I'm going to have to learn to live by the principles found in the other Steps. If I don't, my mental obsession will kill me.

I had to learn to tell the truth. Believe me, that was hard to do. But I found out that when I told the truth, it built my character. Now that's a principle. It pays off. I had to learn to be kind. I learned I could be compassionate, understanding, patient, tolerant. This is a principle, and it builds my character. Now all principles are spiritual. And if they are spiritual, they have an origin. They started somewhere, and today they do the same thing as when they started. It's no different than mathematical principles. If two and two equal four, can you make six out of it? No, the truth is that two and two equal four. You can bank on it. You can use it. You can go through the rest of your life with that principle and it will always do the same thing. This program of recovery is the way it was from the beginning.

▲ How did you finally get the message?

Pain and suffering. Going all the time in the day I was in. All of sudden, it was like getting hit with a two-by-four. You couldn't depend on me then. One time I'd be a ranting, raving madman. Other times I was a beautiful person, at least in the way I acted. I wasn't a beautiful person, but I acted that way. I didn't know what I was doing. I thought that if you just stayed sober and kept going to meetings, eventually you'd come out a winner. I had a great sponsor, believe me. But his application, his God, and his daily reprieve was his own, not mine. In other words, I had great information but I couldn't use it. This is the trouble with every alcoholic who gets here. You are fed some good stuff, but you can't use it. I couldn't use it. But there came a time when my life got to be important to me. And it started with God. From there, it was a process of trying things, failing, falling down, getting up and going on again. At some point, I realized I was hurting people and didn't want to do it no more. I wanted to do something about it. I wanted to grow today. I didn't want to rest on my yesterdays. Now I have a growing life, a good life. This here life is the best life. Right now. It's always prime time.

▲ Have you identified a word or a sentence as a principle that goes with each step?

I found this set somewhere in the literature. It was put out years ago.

> Step 1: Honesty. Fairness and straightforwardness of conduct, adherence to the facts.

Step 2: Hope. To expect with desire something on which hopes are centered.

Step 3: Faith. Complete confidence, belief and trust.

Step 4: Courage. Firmness of mind, and the will in the face of extreme difficulty, mental or moral strength to withstand fear.

Step 5: Integrity. The quality or state of being complete and undivided soundness.

Step 6: Willingness. Prompt to act or respond. Accepted and done of choice or without reluctance.

Step 7: Humility. Not proud or haughty, not arrogant or assertive. Clear and concise understanding of what we are, followed by a sincere desire to become what we can be.

Step 8: Love. Unselfish concern that freely accepts another and seeks his good; to hold dear.

Step 9: Discipline. Training that corrects, molds or perfects the mental faculties or moral character; to bring under control, to train or develop by instruction.

Step 10: Patience and perseverance. Steadfast despite opposition, difficulty, or adversity. Able or willing to bear, to persist in an undertaking in spite of counter-influence.

Step 11: Awareness. Alive and alert, vigilance in observing.

Step 12: Service. A helpful act, contribution to the welfare of others. Useful labor that does not produce a tangible commodity. We practice these principles in all our affairs and carry this message to others.

That was put out years ago. Try applying them. You'll find a world that you didn't know existed. I guarantee it. I'll put it in writing and sign it.

Bibliography

AA Grapevine, Inc., The. *Language of the Heart*, The. New York: The AA Grapevine, Inc., 1988.

Alcoholics Anonymous World Services, Inc. *Alcoholics Anonymous*. 3rd Ed. New York: Alcoholics Anonymous World Services, Inc., 1976.

Alcoholics Anonymous World Services, Inc. *Alcoholics Anonymous Comes of Age: A Brief History of AA*. New York: Alcoholics Anonymous World Services, Inc., 1985.

Alcoholics Anonymous World Services, Inc. *Twelve Steps and Twelve Traditions (Twelve by Twelve)*. New York: Alcoholics Anonymous World Services, Inc., 1952, 1953, 1981.

Fox, Emmet. *The Sermon on the Mount: The Key to Success in Life*. San Francisco: Harper San Francisco, 1966.

Tiebout, Harry M. *Tiebout Collection*. Reprinted from *Quarterly Journal Studies on Alcohol* (1953). Center City, Minn.: Hazelden Foundation, 1990.

PRIMETIME™

RECOVERY

CHANGING LIVES EVERYDAY

Quick Order Form

Fax orders: 310-802-0215. Send this form.

Telephone orders: Call toll free 866-4 RECOVERY (473-2683).
Have your credit card ready.

Email orders: orders@primetimerecovery.com

Postal orders: Primetime Recovery. PO Box 2035,
Manhattan Beach, CA 90266-2035. USA.

Please send me the following books.

____

____

____

Please send me **FREE** information on:

Audio Series Video Series Speaking/seminars

Name ____________________________________

Address __________________________________

City __________________State _____ Zip______-______

Telephone__________________________________

Email address ______________________________

Sales tax: Please add 8% for products shipped to California addresses.

Shipping by air:

US: $4.00 for the first book; $2.00 for each additional product.

International: $9.00 for the first book; $5.00 for each additional product (estimate).

Payment: 1) Check: Make payable to Primetime Recovery

2) Credit Card: Visa Mastercard American Express

Card number: ______________________________

Name on Card: ____________________Exp Date:___/___

Signature of cardholder: ________________________

PRIMETIME™

RECOVERY

CHANGING LIVES EVERYDAY

Quick Order Form

Fax orders: 310-802-0215. Send this form.

Telephone orders: Call toll free 866-4 RECOVERY (473-2683).
Have your credit card ready.

Email orders: orders@primetimerecovery.com

Postal orders: Primetime Recovery. PO Box 2035,
Manhattan Beach, CA 90266-2035. USA.

Please send me the following books.

____

____

____

Please send me **FREE** information on:

Audio Series   Video Series   Speaking/seminars

Name ____

Address ______________________________________

City ____________________ State _____ Zip______-______

Telephone ____________________________________

Email address _________________________________

Sales tax: Please add 8% for products shipped to California addresses.

Shipping by air:

US: $4.00 for the first book; $2.00 for each additional product.

International: $9.00 for the first book; $5.00 for each additional product (estimate).

Payment: 1) Check: Make payable to Primetime Recovery

2) Credit Card: Visa   Mastercard   American Express

Card number: ___________________________________

Name on Card: ____________________ Exp Date:___/___

Signature of cardholder: ____________________________

PRIMETIME™
RECOVERY

CHANGING LIVES EVERYDAY

Quick Order Form

Fax orders: 310-802-0215. Send this form.

Telephone orders: Call toll free 866-4 RECOVERY (473-2683).
Have your credit card ready.

Email orders: orders@primetimerecovery.com

Postal orders: Primetime Recovery. PO Box 2035,
Manhattan Beach, CA 90266-2035. USA.

Please send me the following books.

____

____

____

Please send me **FREE** information on:

Audio Series Video Series Speaking/seminars

Name ____

Address ______________________________________

City ____________________State ____ Zip_____-_____

Telephone ______________________________________

Email address ___________________________________

Sales tax: Please add 8% for products shipped to California addresses.

Shipping by air:

US: $4.00 for the first book; $2.00 for each additional product.
International: $9.00 for the first book; $5.00 for each additional product (estimate).

Payment: 1) Check: Make payable to Primetime Recovery
2) Credit Card: Visa Mastercard American Express

Card number: ___________________________________

Name on Card: ____________________Exp Date:___/___

Signature of cardholder: ____________________________

PRIMETIME™

RECOVERY

CHANGING LIVES EVERYDAY

Quick Order Form

Fax orders: 310-802-0215. Send this form.

Telephone orders: Call toll free 866-4 RECOVERY (473-2683).
Have your credit card ready.

Email orders: orders@primetimerecovery.com

Postal orders: Primetime Recovery. PO Box 2035,
Manhattan Beach, CA 90266-2035. USA.

Please send me the following books.

____

____

____

Please send me **FREE** information on:

Audio Series Video Series Speaking/seminars

Name ____________________________________

Address __________________________________

City __________________State _____ Zip______-______

Telephone_________________________________

Email address _____________________________

Sales tax: Please add 8% for products shipped to California addresses.

Shipping by air:

US: $4.00 for the first book; $2.00 for each additional product.

International: $9.00 for the first book; $5.00 for each additional product (estimate).

Payment: 1) Check: Make payable to Primetime Recovery

2) Credit Card: Visa Mastercard American Express

Card number: ______________________________

Name on Card: ________________________Exp Date:___/___

Signature of cardholder: ________________________